WHOM GOD HAS MADE CLEAN

A PRONOMIAN
POCKET GUIDE TO
ACTS 10:9-15

R. M. BAILEY

Whom God Has Made Clean: A Pronomian Pocket Guide to Acts 10:9–15

Pronomian Publishing LLC
Clover, SC 29710

ISBN: 979-8-9908630-3-3

To God, who alone cleanses us all in Christ.

And to Judah Hartman, whose godly love, faith, and obedience made the writing of this book, among many other things, possible.

CONTENTS

PREFACE

In November of 2023, I independently published a short book titled *What God Hath Created: Does the New Testament Do Away with the Dietary Commandments?* The motivation behind the work was simple—to provide an accessible yet thorough apologia for the continuity of the Law by way of addressing difficult and contentious passages throughout the New Testament concerning the dietary regulations. The work was successful to some degree, even convincing a Southern Baptist pastor that the dietary laws, at least, continue to have an ongoing role in the believer's life! The present work serves as both a *narrowing* and *enlarging* continuation of that argument, tailor made for Pronomian Publishing's *Pronomian Pocket Guide* series—a collection full of promise and sure to provide the Messianic community, and the church at large, with short, accessible, and immensely helpful treatments of the topic of the Law and its relevance post-Cross.

What does it mean to say that this work is both more narrow and enlarged compared to my previous book? By "narrowing," I mean that instead of taking a wide brush approach to the topic—one which requires a relatively massive treatment, and which my earlier work did not attempt to accomplish—the goal here is to focus on one section of Scripture: Peter's vision in Acts 10. Equally so, by "narrowing" I mean focusing (almost) purely on a textual approach to Peter's vision. This approach has its benefits as well as its limitations, which leads to the "enlarging." By enlarging, I mean the fact that any recorded event, person, etc., recorded in Scripture comes with a plethora of motifs, tropes, significances, and textual parallels that color in the lines of what we read. To put it another way, every text of the Bible has an entire background of endless information and concepts which surround what is being said and illuminates what is being expressed.

An Appetizer-Sized Study of Acts 10

Just as the animals in Peter's vision were lowered down on a sheet, so too is the vision of Acts 10 itself lowered to us—the readers—upon a tapestry woven with themes of Law, ecclesiology, eschatology, and theology. Examples include God's unfolding plan for mankind, the salvation provided to us through Christ, the concept of covenant, the future permanent dwelling of God, the division between Jew and Gentile, and the list will go on. With this being said, what we read in Acts 10 is not limited to the words on parchments and papyti that have been translated into our Bibles; it also encompasses the echoes and fulfillments of God's Grand Story, woven throughout the fabric of Scripture from Genesis to Revelation.

To encapsulate *all* of these details and nuances warrants a work well beyond the limited scope of this book. These things—what we may call a "broader biblical theology"—serve as the entrée (food pun intended) of the meal. But what comes first is the appetizer: what the text plainly says. Thus, this present work—both extending the existing conversation while leaving the rest for another day—is meant to provide the reader with that first course: does the vision in Acts 10 depict God's cleansing of unclean animals? And if so, is that consistent with (a) the Old Testament influence upon the vision, (b) the contextual and textual nature of the vision, and (c) the remainder of the

New Testament's attitude and views on the dietary laws and the Law in general? This is the focus and the essence of this work. By focusing exclusively on the vision, we can peel back the layers and test both the popular view and the objections, all from a position of the Law's larger continuity—the harmony between the First and Second Testaments.

A Preview of the Meal Ahead

The structure and flow of this book is thus quite simple. In Chapter 1, we will survey the topic of the Law, Jew-Gentile relationships, Jesus's view of the Law, and information immediately relevant to the discussion. Let us call this our "setting of the table." Following this, we will spend the next chapter focusing on the text of Acts 10 itself. Once we have thoroughly analyzed Peter's vision in Acts 10, we will finish off the book with the conclusion. In the conclusion, we briefly synthesize our findings, speculate on various implications for other passages as well as a larger view of the Law and the believer, and tie together the whole work with concluding thoughts.

Given the accessible nature of this work, the reader will find much of the heavier material—let us call this "the meat"—within the footnotes. These footnotes will, at times, refer the reader to sources better fit to handle the necessary primary and secondary information. The demand of such a topic extends well beyond what is immediately set before us, and for further theological, soteriological, and doctrinal details, I will refer the reader to my recent work, *Neither Circumcision Nor Uncircumcision: A Messianic & Exegetical Commentary on the Book of Galatians* (Independent, 2023), abbreviated as *NCNU*, where I tackle the entirety of Paul's theology, and especially his view(s) towards the Law.

As another contribution to the *Pronomian Pocket Guide* series, my hope and prayer is that this work is not only enlightening and convincing to you, the reader, but also that it encourages us all to learn. We all are equally students of God's Holy and Precious Word given to us—the gift second only to the gift of salvation found in Jesus Christ, and in Jesus Christ alone. And even more, I also pray that this work, in some way, pushes us all to dig deeper into not just the Bible but also into a deeper, obedient, and loving relationship with God our Creator—the Creator who has not made *what* is inherently unclean clean, but who has made those *who* are inherently unclean clean. And *whom* God has made clean, let no one call common.

CHAPTER 1

SETTING THE TABLE

Do the dietary commandments of the Old Testament (OT) apply to the modern-day believer? For most, the immediate answer would be a resounding "no!" But how well thought out is that answer? Most believers come to this conclusion based on what they've been taught—whether from peers, the pulpit, or the various voices surrounding them. But the question remains: have they truly grappled with the inquiry itself? This idea didn't emerge in a vacuum. Many New Testament (NT) passages appear to suggest that the Law has been annulled in Christ—texts such as Mark 7:19, Acts 15, Romans 14, and Colossians 2:16–17, among others. For many Christians, the matter seems settled. However, in the scholarly realm, the answer is not so straightforward. Of all topics that have occupied the focus of scholars, the Law is at the top of the list. And why is that?

Answering this question thoroughly demands a treatment well beyond the scope of this present work—and, in truth, such an undertaking often involves more time distilling misunderstandings than it does simply presenting a proper interpretation. In many cases, one must "unlearn" before they can truly "learn." And behind most claims that the Law has been abrogated lies a chest of presuppositions, dogmatic commitments, and common misunderstandings. This is, in part, a consequence of the general famine of biblical knowledge in our present day. One could argue that biblical literacy is at an all-time low, with sound biblical education largely confined to formal institutions. The irony, of course, is that we now have more access to biblical resources and information than ever before in history—yet, in spite of this abundance, the famine persists. Put simply, we often tend to cling to what we've been taught, and seldom do we examine the Word for what it actually says.

This is hardly a novel problem. Certainly, this problem has plagued every human since the very beginning and is no respecter of persons. Pedigree, education, intelligence, and the like offer no protection from the tendency to elevate personal opinion or tradition above fact. This is simply another consequence of sin, and all too often, we are our own worst enemies. What should concern us is the impact our presuppositions have on us. What we already think about something naturally impresses itself upon how we read, watch, learn, or interpret anything related to it. The question we must ask ourselves is whether we are being objective in how we are handling the data. If most were honest, they would admit that, when it comes to the Law and its applicability today, they have never really given it much thought.

Scripture has virtually every answer we need, but it comes with a built-in clause. As Peter proclaimed, no prophecy is of private interpretation (2 Pet. 1:20), and while this speaks of prophecy, by implication it includes all Scripture. Similarly, the Bereans tested everything that Paul said by measuring it against Scripture (Acts 17:11), and Paul instructed Timothy to study to show oneself approved, properly dividing the Word of Truth (2 Tim. 2:15). Scripture itself commissions us to study its words and not just take interpretations, even our own, at face value. Despite these guiding principles, much of the church maintains the position that the Law no longer applies, and therefore, ought to be abandoned.

Peter's vision in Acts 10 retains a unique position within the debate over the Law and, more generally, modern-day interpretations of Scripture. While the vast majority of Christian voices view this vision as abrogating the food laws, the text itself fails to provide any evidence towards this widely held interpretation. As we will bring up frequently in this book, Scripture clearly and emphatically states that the vision refers to the cleansing of *Gentiles*. At no point—whether implicitly or explicitly—does the text suggest that the vision refers *also* to the cleansing of unclean animals. Such a detail cannot be overstated, for the vision serves as the quintessential example of Christendom superimposing an interpretation upon the text which, to be frank, simply does not exist. Views towards the Vision are not a consequence of sound exegesis and the application of proper hermeneutical method but, rather, wholesale interpolation. This interpolation is so deeply engrained in the Christian readers' mind that a contrary view is often disregarded without even considering the argument. Scholar David B. Woods summarizes the situation aptly:

> The long-term and widespread propagation of the traditional
> dual interpretation of Peter's vision has become so deeply
> ingrained in the collective Christian psyche that it is difficult
> to challenge, regardless of the evidence. Yet, there is nothing
> in this passage (Acts 10:1–11:18) to support the argument
> that the Law is done away with, nor that Peter's vision was
> an injunction by God to forsake the food commandments.
> On the contrary, the text repeatedly affirms that the vision
> was about God's cleansing of the Gentiles. This passage, and
> specifically the vision it describes, does not address the Law at
> all.[1]

As plain as the inquisitive mind could ask for, Peter provides the interpretation of the vision in Acts 10:28: "but God has shown me

---

1   David B. Woods, "Interpreting Peter's Vision in Acts 10:9–16," *Conspectus* 13.1 (2012), 209.

that I should not call any person common or unclean." Additionally, the early Church did not appeal to Acts 10 as a basis for abrogating the dietary laws.[2] So, why does the antinomian interpretation persist? While we can only speculate, I would argue that, beyond the tendency to approach the text with "dogmatic baggage," many believers read the Bible through the lens of a highly-developed and complex web of fallacies and presuppositions. That is, we build our interpretive approach on unstable grounds. Thus, the framework through which we read any given passage is unduly slanted towards a position that sees the Law as oppressive, abrogated, and irrelevant to the modern-day believer.

For most believers, "reading in context" means something like reading the paragraph, preceding and proceeding chapters, or the whole book. However, this is merely the immediate context. What remains is what we can call the "larger context"—the who, what, when, where, why, and how of the Bible. Who is the author writing to? What is the letter about? When is this? Where is this? Why is he writing? How is he writing? In each of these questions there exists a milieu of data: cultural backgrounds, literary devices, religious understandings, political and social dynamics, specific vocabulary, and the list could go on and on. Just as our views of Acts 10 did not come about in a vacuum, neither did the NT. Instead, it interacts with, draws from, builds upon, and springs out of a wealth of background information so deep and dense that one could hardly skim the surface of it in a hundred lifetimes.

What is the point? My point here is that fallacious suppositions naturally and subconsciously superimpose themselves upon our readings of Acts 10 and hinder our ability to properly read Peter's vision contextually. Thus, the goal of this present work is to read Acts 10:9–16 and its surrounding material in its immediate *and* its larger context. In

---

2   Woods, "Interpreting Peter's Vision," 207.

order to prepare the reader, we first have to address the larger context. To do so, we will touch on a few key points that "set the table" of the background behind the NT writings. Given our limitations, we will give brief (re-)contextualizations of the Law and Jewish salvation, Jewish-Gentile relations in the first-century, and Jesus's view of the Law. Finally, we will also touch on the important and enigmatic pericope of Mark 7, where it is claimed that Jesus "cleansed all foods"—a statement that has become the seedbed from which antinomian interpretations of other passages have sprung. By covering these aspects of biblical theology and NT interpretation, we can better situate the conversation going forward.

The Law

The Law is easily one of the most misunderstood topics of the Bible, and understandably so. To the modern believer, it can often seem weird at times.[3] Nevertheless, many people make confident assertions about it—claiming that it is a system of legalistic salvation, oppression, and statutes limited to the physical nation of Israel. We will address these three claims in reverse order.

---

3 Especially Leviticus. As Bryan D. Bibb puts it, one "encounters in Leviticus a text that is fractured and ambiguous" (*Ritual Words and Narrative Worlds in the Book of Leviticus* [Edinburgh: T&T Clark, 2008], 165). Gerald A. Klingbeil comments that this is mostly "due to the fact that it was presupposed that the reader would have instinctively known the involved language" of ritual and, thus, the modern reader "must work much harder in order to discover the underlying concepts and understand the (often) abbreviated nature of the ritual" ("Altars, Ritual and Theology: Preliminary Thoughts on the Importance of Cult and Ritual for a Theology of the Hebrew Scriptures," *VT* 54.4 [2004], 513, 514). The entire "worldview" and "presupposed knowledge" of Leviticus is entirely foreign to us. This holds true for the remainder of the OT Law.

Boundary Markers for Israel

The popular view holds that a central function of Law was to set Israel apart from the surrounding nations. Thus, the commandments in the Law served as "boundary markers." The difficulty here is that there is significant overlap between customs and practices within the ancient Near Eastern (ANE) civilizations and Israel's own. Perhaps the best example is that two commandments that would seem to physically distinguish Israel—circumcision and tassels—were more or less practiced by Israel's neighbors. Circumcision, for instance, was found to be practiced in numerous other civilizations.[4] Moreover, Jacob Milgrom has demonstrated that the commandment for tassels (*tzitzit*) in Numbers 15:37–71 was not exactly unique to Israel, as the practice is well attested in reliefs uncovered in archaeological digs.[5] Given the symbolism of royalty behind the color, "The blue [*tekêleth*] thread reminded [the Israelite] that he belonged to 'a kingdom of priests and a holy nation' (Exod. 19:6),"[6] quite in line with them being a set-apart nation. But the tassels themselves likely would do little to distinguish Israel from her neighbors.

Parallels abound between the Code of Hammurabi and the Law of Moses;[7] glaring similarities can be seen between Israel's tabernacle

---

4   This observation entered the biblical scholarly conversation as early as Jack M. Sasson, "Circumcision in the Ancient Near East," *JBL* 85.4 (1966), 473–476.

5   Jacob Milgrom, "Of Hems and Tassels: Rank, Authority and Holiness Were Expressed in Antiquity by Fringes on Garments," *BAR* 9.3 (1983), 61–65. Milgrom was not, however, the first to notice this correlation. For depictions, see Milgrom's article as well as https://www.patternsofevidence.com/2020/12/18/hems-of-garments-and-him/.

6   Gordon J. Wenham, *Numbers: An Introduction and Commentary*, TCOT (Downers Grove, IL: InterVarsity Press, 2008), 21f.

7   David Wright, *Inventing God's Law: How the Covenant Code of the Bible Used and Revised the Laws of Hammurabi* (Oxford: Oxford University Press, 2013).

and other temples in both architecture and symbolism;[8] and even the sacrificial system shares several features with those of surrounding cultures.[9] Prohibitions against the consumption of certain animals—such as pigs, donkeys, horses, and mules—as well as prohibitions against them coming into the vicinity of sacred space (i.e., temples) were also present in the ancient world, though they differed in various ways from those outlined in the Law of Moses.[10] Generally speaking, ideas surrounding im/purity and defilement reflect conventional views of the time,[11] and the prescriptions surrounding women and menstruation find close parallels to practices found in other ancient cultures.[12] Even the specific law prescribing different durations of impurity for women based on whether they gave birth to a male or female baby can be found in other cultures.[13] This is not to throw weight behind critical

8   G. K. Beale, *The Temple and the Church's Mission: A Biblical Theology of the Dwelling Place of God*, NSBT 17 (Downers Grove, IL: IVP Academic, 2004), 29–122, esp. 50–59; 87–92.

9   See my own treatment on the Temple cult in its function, meaning, and (lack of) similarity to ANE practices in the aside "The Temple Cult and Sacrifice" in *NCNU*, 293–314.

10   Max D. Price, *Evolution of a Taboo: Pigs and People in the Ancient Near East* (Oxford: Oxford University Press, 2021). See also Elias J. Bickerman, "A Seleucid Proclamation Concerning the Temple in Jerusalem" in *Studies in Jewish and Christian History*, AJEC 68. Vol. 1 (Leiden: Brill, 2007), 366.

11   Yitzhaq Feder, "Defilement, Disgust, and Disease: The Experiential Basis of Hittite and Akkadian Terms for Iniquity," *JAOS* 136.1 (2016), 99–116; idem., "The Semantics of Purity in the Ancient Near East: Lexical Meaning as a Projection of Embodied Existence," *JANER* 14 (2014), 87–113.

12   Marten Stol, *Women in the Ancient Near East* (Boston: Berlin: De Gruyter, 2016), 517–520.

13   Jacob Milgrom, *Leviticus 1–16*, AYB (New Haven, CT: Yale University Press, 1998), 742–765, esp. 750–1; 763–765.

views of the OT, but simply to demonstrate that much of the Law was by no means *novel* (though it was certainly *correct*).

While the Law did make Israel distinct to some degree, many of its practices were quite similar to those of their neighbors'. The real distinction is found within the *wisdom* and *truth* contained in God's Law. As we read in Deuteronomy 4:6, the nations would be enamored by this divine revelation: "Keep them and do them, for that will be your wisdom and your understanding in the sight of the peoples, who, when they hear all these statutes, will say, 'Surely this great nation is a wise and understanding people.'" The Law, handed down by creation's Maker, would demonstrate the wisdom of Israel's God, establishing Israel as the only valid possessors of divine instruction—and truly, a legitimate priestly nation called to extend God's wisdom and truth to the nations.[14]

It is true that the Law was given to set the Israelites apart from the nations, but not in the way that it is often understood. For example, in Exodus 19:5–6 God declares that Israel must keep the Law because God has set them apart as a holy nation and kingdom of priests. Similarly, Leviticus 20:26 states, "You shall be holy to me, for I the LORD am holy and have separated you from the peoples, that you should be mine." In separating them from the nations as a holy people, the Law is given so that they may mirror God's own holiness. Essentially, Israel is given the Law for the explicit purpose of being holy, rather than unholy like the nations. The word used in Leviticus 20:26 for "separated," *bâdal*, indeed conveys the sense of distinguishing or

---

14   For the centrifugal aspects and universal inclusion in the Abrahamic covenant and the Law within Israel-nations relationship, see Walter J. Kaiser Jr., *Mission in the Old Testament: Israel as a Light to the Nations* (Grand Rapids, MI: Baker Academic, 2012), 32–35.

differentiating between things—removing something from what is common. But the suggestion that the Law served solely to distinguish Israel, and thus does not apply to the universal Church, is somewhat anachronistic. Just as the Law was given at Sinai when God brought Israel out of Egypt—setting them apart as his own—so too do we receive instruction on holiness through the Spirit and the NT when we come to Christ, setting us apart from the world.

The Law as Oppressive and Impossible

Properly understood, the Law was the Creator's instruction to a nation he was creating. The very word translated as "law," *tôrâh*, ought to be understood as "instruction," "guidance," or even "journey" in the sense of "direction."[15] God gave specific instructions on worship, work, and life—that is essentially what the Law is. The notion that the Law is an oppressive system of impossible-to-keep commandments is a modern misconception; it is not rooted in an understanding of what the Law was or how it functioned. How could King David speak so worshipfully about the Law in the Psalms (e.g., Ps. 19:7–14) if it were merely a dry, mechanical, and oppressive system? Rather, the Law describes God's instructions for living amongst him, people, and the creation. If one were to observe every superficial problem in the world today, it would quickly become apparent that observance of the Law would essentially solve most—if not all—of them.

---

15   William L. Holloday defines *tôrâh* firstly as "direction, instruction," and then as "law" (ed., CHALOT [Grand Rapids, MI: Eerdmans, 1988], 388). The word originates from the verb *yârâ'*, which means "to shoot" or "to point." For "Journey," see Ivana Procházková, *The Torah/Law is a Journey: Using Cognitive and Culturally Oriented Linguistics to Interpret and Translate Metaphors in the Hebrew Bible* (Prague: Karolinum Press, 2022).

The Law frequently reveals some type of divine understanding of nature itself,[16] with details that would be realized only by future generations and through more technical and scientific advancements. For our purposes, this is particularly interesting with respect to the food laws, as Scripture provides no explanation for their purpose and scholars struggle to find one. A simple answer is that these animals just aren't meant for food. That the prohibited land animals and birds are predatory suggests that the dietary prohibitions align with the course of nature. This pattern extends to marine life as well, where bottom feeders (lobsters, crabs, shrimp, etc.) are placed into the category of unclean (Lev. 11; Deut. 14). While we can only speculate on the reasons behind these distinctions, one thing is clear—the Law does not take (textual) shape as an oppressive system.[17]

---

16 One such example is that of fallowing the Land every seventh year, which has remarkable benefits to soil health, water management, and specifically prevents the growth of fungi and pests. See D.C. Nielsen, Franciso J. Calderón, "Fallow Effects on Soil," in *Soil Management: Building a Stable Base for Agriculture,* ed. Jerry L. Hatfield, Thomas J. Sauer, eds. (Madison, WI: American Society of Agronomy, 2011), 287–301. See also Jeremy Cusimano, "Study Finds Land Fallowing Improves Soil Quality in PVID," *Water Resource Quarterly* 22.1 (2014), 1–4; Abigail Klein Leichman, "SHMITA: The Israeli Farmers Who Are Giving Their Land a Year's Rest - Jewish Ledger,," *Jewish Ledger* 3 (Sept. 2021), www.jewishledger.com/2021/09/shmita-the-israeli-farmers-who-are-giving-their-land-a-years-rest. Other examples of the Bible's unique understanding of nature abound, and at every turn one encounters some type of obvious divine inspiration, particularly with the Law. This is not to say, however, that the Bible is a science book. Such an approach has led to much fruitless (and sometimes embarrassing) discussion.

17 The comparison of the Law with wisdom is important to note. See Craig G. Bartolomew and Ryan P. O'Dowd, *Old Testament Wisdom Literature: A Theological Introduction* (Downers Grove, IL: IVP Academic, 2011), 286–304. See also the recent work by JiSeong J. Kwon, Seth A. Bledsoe, eds., *Between Wisdom and Torah: Discourses on Wisdom and Law in Second Temple Judaism*, DCL 51 (Berlin: De Gruyter, 2023).

Even a retributive system—where one "gets what they give," analogous to legalism—finds no place in Scripture. Looking to Qoheleth (Ecclesiastes) and Job, we see a direct challenge to this idea. God's explicit rebuke of Job and his friends exposes their retributive worldview as inappropriate and a misrepresentation of his character (Job 42:7).[18] Qoheleth's comments in Ecclesiastes 7:15–20 further dismiss the notion of a strict retribution economy.[19] And Proverbs, "Taken as a whole…by no means represents a mechanical, automatic character-consequence understanding of retribution."[20]

Moreover, the idea of a legalistic system enumerated by 613 commandments is a late tradition.[21] Likewise, the division of the Law into "moral," "ceremonial," and "civil," is a dogmatic fabrication that neither finds support nor synchronicity in either testament. As Richard E. Averbeck remarks, "even if one divides the laws into moral, civil, and ceremonial categories, the New Testament cites and applies specific laws and principles from all three categories to the life of the church and the believer."[22] The transmission of the Law is so

---

18 See Lennart Boström: "God's words in the epilogue constitute the final blow to a legalistic application of the retribution principle in the Old Testament" ("Retribution and Wisdom Literature," in *Interpreting Old Testament Wisdom Literature*, ed. David G. Firth, Lindsay Wilson [Downers Grove, IL: IVP Academic, 2017], 148).

19 In v. 20 Qoheleth sees that nobody goes without sinning, but here he dismantles (for us) the idea of sure retribution, which would be an inevitable result of a retribution system. See Choon-Leong Seow, *Ecclesiastes: A New Translation with Introduction and Commentary*, AYB (New Haven: Yale University Press, 1997), 252–258, 266–270). See also Thomas Kruger, *Qoheleth: A Commentary on the Book of Qoheleth*, Hermenia (Augsburg: Fortress Press, 2004), 135–139.

20 Bartholomew and O'Dowd, *Wisdom Literature*, 271.

21 For the history, see Albert D. Friedberg, *Crafting the 613 Commandments: Maimonides on the Enumeration, Classification and Formulation of the Scriptural Commandments* (Boston: Academic Studies Press, 2013).

22 Richard E. Averbeck, *The Old Testament Law for the Life of the Church: Reading the Torah*

wildly varied, with different "types" of commandments placed closely together—and often overlapping, harmonizing, and carrying multiple meanings—that attempting either (a) to enumerate the entire corpus or (b) to divide it neatly into distinct categories demands such a degree of interpretive gymnastics and questionable systematizing that it is difficult for an honest reader to accept.

A "Works-Salvation" System of Legalism

Perhaps more importantly, the view of life under the Law as a legalistic existence is, unfortunately, a false caricature—one that has had lasting and terrible impacts, much of which has been ingrained in the Christian mindset through Lutheran and Reformed frameworks. On this, Daniel I. Block writes the following:

> Luther tended to read them [the texts of Deuteronomy]
> through Paul's rhetorical and seemingly antinomian state-
> ments…and his own debilitating experience of works-righ-
> teousness within the Roman Catholic church. Hence, he saw
> a radical contrast between the law (which kills) and the gospel
> (which gives life). His emphasis on the dual function of the
> law (civic—to maintain external order on earth; theologi-
> cal—to convict people of sin and drive them to Christ; cf.
> Lohse 270–74) missed the point of Deuteronomy. This book
> presents the law as a gift to guide the redeemed in righteous-
> ness, leading to life.[23]

---

in the Light of Christ (Downers Grove, IL: IVP Academic, 2022), 14.

23   Daniel I. Block, "Deuteronomy," in *Theological Interpretation of the Old Testament: A Book-by-Book Survey*, ed. Kevin J. Vanhoozer (Grand Rapids, MI: Baker Academic, 2008), 58.

Likewise, J. N. Oswalt helpfully points out the following:

> [O]bedience to the commands of the covenant was never
> intended to be a way into a relationship with God. Instead,
> such obedience was expected to be a glad response to the
> revelation of God's grace in His deliverance from bondage...
> Holy living is the necessary and natural outcome of a genuine
> experience of God's grace. The concept of the law that Jesus
> and Paul both attacked so vehemently, that by obedience one
> could earn God's favor, is neither the Pentateuch's nor the
> OT's. It is a Pharisaic perversion.[24]

Oswalt's last comments, however, are misguided. In recent decades
the idea of ancient Jews achieving salvation by works has largely fallen
out of favor within the scholarly world. This shift is mostly attributed
to the landmark volume *Paul and Palestinian Judaism* by E. P. Sanders,
which, surveying Jewish literature with the NT, began to overturn
such views. Sanders's proposals, having been (almost) virtually unanimously accepted, gave birth to what is called the *New Paul Perspective*,
championed by others such as James D. G. Dunn and N. T. Wright.
On Sanders' findings and implications, John M. G. Barclay explains
it well:

> His results were sufficient to challenge and eventually over-
> turn the misrepresentation of Judaism commonly found in
> Christian-influenced scholarship. It is no longer intellectually

---

24   J. N. Oswalt, "Theology of the Pentateuch," in *Dictionary of the Old Testament: Pentateuch,*
ed. T. Desmond Alexander and David W. Baker (Downers Grove, IL: IVP Academic,
2003), 858.

defensible to represent ancient Judaism as a religion of "legalism" or "works-righteousness," as if Jews sought to "earn" salvation by doing good works. That caricature must count as one of the many anti-Jewish tropes that have circulated in Christian-influenced scholarship but must now be strongly repudiated.[25]

Similarly, James D. G. Dunn adds that now that this idea has been shown to be false, "Nothing less became necessary than a complete reassessment of Paul's relationship with his ancestral religion, not to mention all the considerable consequences which were bound to follow for our contemporary understanding of his theology."[26] While there are passages shrouded in ambiguity, especially in Paul's corpus, which we are unable to address here, the reader is encouraged to note this shift in biblical scholarship. Why is this important? Because if Paul wasn't writing against Jews who sought to earn salvation by keeping the Law, *then what was he writing against exactly?* This is the million-dollar question. If we find no blatant and consistent legalism in Jewish literature, we must reexamine how we have read the OT, Gospels, and Paul's literature.

The idea that legalism formed the base of Jewish existence with God prior to Calvary is largely rooted in post-canonical writings and a misunderstanding of the OT Law itself. A crucial trend was the Church's increasingly Gentile identity and the false representation of Judaism as a legalistic religion during the first few centuries of Chris-

---

25 John M. G. Barclay, *Paul and the Power of Grace* (Grand Rapids, MI: Eerdmans, 2020), 53.

26 James D. G. Dunn, *The Theology of Paul the Apostle* (Grand Rapids, MI: Eerdmans, 2006), 5.

tianity—an era in which many of these writers held and expressed antisemitic ideas. The idea of "law" as we conceive of it today would not have been held by ancient Israelites, and the conception of the Law into a more formalized "legal" system has a long and convoluted trail.[27] One point we may consider is how ancient Israelites adhered to a legalistic, by-the-book existence prior to the rediscovery of the Torah in 2 Kings 22. For the Israelite, enjoined to the collective psyche was a religion of covenant and ritual rather than any type of legalism. Modern readers often misunderstand the context of passages like Isaiah 29:13 in Mark 7:6–7 as connoting legalism rather than, properly, religious-worship prescriptions.[28] That Jesus specifically regards the Pharisees as "lawless" throughout the Gospels—and in Mark saying that they "leave" (*aphentes*), "reject" (*atheteite*), and "annul" (*akurountes*)[29] the commandments in order to "hold fast"[30] to their traditions— would seem to distill such a view. How can one be "lawless" if they are "legalists?"

---

27 Anne Fitzpatrick-McKinley, *The Transformation of Torah from Scribal Advice to Law* LHBOTS 287 (Sheffield: Sheffield Academic Press, 1999); Michael LeFebvre, *Collections, Codes, and Torah: The Re-Characterization of Israel's Written Law*, LHBOTS 451 (New York: T&T Clark, 2006); John J. Collins, *The Invention of Judaism: Torah and Jewish Identity from Deuteronomy to Paul* (Berkeley: University of California Press, 2017); idem., "The Transformation of the Torah in Second Temple Judaism," *JSJ* 45.4 (2012): 455–474.

28 See especially Hans Wilderberger, *Isaiah 28–39: A Continental Commentary*, trans. Thomas H. Trapp (Minneapolis: Fortress Press, 2002), 89–90.

29 See David M. Young and Michael Strickland: "Through the figure of climax, the sentences seem to 'climb higher and higher,' adding power to the charge" (*The Rhetoric of Jesus in the Gospel of Mark* [Minneapolis: Fortress Press, 2017], 202–203).

30 According to Robert H. Gundry, "holding fast" has covenantal undertones (*Mark: A Commentary on His Apology for the Cross* [Grand Rapids, MI: Eerdmans, 1993], 351). I would add that *tēreō* ("guard," 7:9) does, too.

The covenant-ritual-cultic aspect of Israelite religion is important to understand. Seth Schwartz proposes that the paradigm of Israel's religion, extending into the Second Temple period, was structured around God-Temple-Torah, with the second category, the Temple, seldom impressing upon the reader.[31] As I write elsewhere:

> The Old Covenant system had an established relief for when
> people inevitably sinned and fell short of God's Holiness (i.e.,
> the entire sacrificial system). It would seem incompatible
> for God to expect perfect obedience while simultaneously
> creating a system for the exact opposite inevitably happening
> (sin). Further, the sacrificial system was part of the Law, so
> for one to truly keep the Law for salvation this would include
> adhering to the ordinances prescribed for shortcoming of sin.
> The standard demanded by God cannot be to never sin since
> He establishes a system to cover this.[32]

To think that the ancient Israelite or Second-Temple-Period Jew would not write within the shadow of the Temple is unimaginable. To be sure, the Temple—much like our Cross—stood as the source for their salvation and the symbol of their assurance. This sentiment, held by Israelites, is echoed in Jeremiah 7:4–10 where God says, "Do not trust in these deceptive words: 'This is the Temple of The Lord, the Temple of The Lord, the Temple of the Lord'" and calls out their wickedness, adding, "Behold, you trust in deceptive words to no avail." He asks the elucidatory question, "Will you steal, murder, commit

---

31 Seth Schwartz, *Imperialism and Jewish Society: 200 B.C.E to 640 C.E.* (Princeton, NJ: Princeton University Press, 2001), 49.
32 *NCNU*, 29.

adultery, swear falsely, make offerings to Baal, and go after other gods that you have not known, and then come and stand before me in this house, which is called by my name, and say, 'We are delivered!', only to go on committing all of these abominations?"

Since God was present in their midst and forgiving their sins via the Temple system, the people to whom Jeremiah spoke assumed they were in good standing—even as they lived completely contrary to what God expected from them. This path would eventually lead to their punishment, the Exile, which some argue is itself the substance of the covenant curses.[33] Statements throughout the OT that appear to reject feasts, Sabbaths, and sacrifices are often used to suggest that God took no delight in them. However, this interpretation overlooks the idolatrous environment in which these rebukes were made and the divine response to that unfaithfulness.[34] Such a mechanical and superficial religion would not work with God (cf. Isa. 29:13), nor would it work for the people. However, the very fact that Israel held to this flawed mindset suggests that such an economy was never at play.

As Logan Williams has said recently on the first episode of his and Paul Sloan's *Jesus and Jewish Law* podcast, if God expected absolute perfection according to the Law, and only gave it to demonstrate man's inability to keep to his perfect standard, "this kind of portrays God

---

33   Most notably N. T. Wright. See James M. Scott, *Exile: A Conversation with N. T. Wright* (Downers Grove, IL: IVP Academic, 2017).

34   See Thomas R. Schreiner: "The prophets declaim against superstitious or mechanical offering of sacrifices (e.g., Isa. 1:11–13; Jer. 6:20; 7:21–23; Hosea 6:6; Amos 4:4–5; 5:22–24; Mic. 6:6). Formerly, many scholars maintained that the prophets rejected sacrifices altogether, but it is generally recognized now that they did not repudiate sacrifices and offerings per se but criticized a mechanical, external, superficial, and magical view of sacrifices, as if sacrifices could atone even if they were offered with a wrong attitude (cf. Prov. 15:8; 21:3, 7)" (*The King in His Beauty: A Biblical Theology of the Old and New Testaments* [Grand Rapids, MI: Baker Academic, 2013], 55).

as… the ultimate gas lighter." Much of this confusion comes by way of Lutheran perspectives but also misunderstanding Paul's various statements. Again, while beyond our scope to delve into Paul's writings, how do we make sense of Paul's statements like that to the Philippians where he was "blameless" (*amemptos*) according to the Law (Phil. 3:6)? Peter T. O'Brien writes that Paul is describing a "righteousness which is 'in the law', is 'rooted in the law', or 'rests in the law.'" As he goes on to say, "Clearly this is no pessimistic self-portrait or recollection of one tortured by an unattainable ideal, a conclusion that has often been drawn from Rom. 7. Here is a man well satisfied, reminiscent of the young rich ruler in the Gospel story (Lk. 18:21) who claims to have kept all the commandments from his youth."[35] Commenting on Paul's words in Galatians 3, along with the ambiguous "works of the law" phrase,[36] Dunn writes the following:

> Most attempt to resolve the riddle by reading in a further
> assumption of Paul: that 'those who rely on works of the law'
> means those who seek to achieve their own righteousness
> before God; and that in quoting Deut. xxvii.26 Paul presup-
> posed that it is impossible to fulfill all that the law requires
> (the 'all' is found only in LXX, not in the Hebrew). The
> hidden presumption is that complete or perfect obedience to
> the law is beyond human capacity: however zealous any might
> be, they fail to abide by everything written in the law, and so
> fall under its curse. The problem for this reading is twofold.
> (1) We have already seen that Paul's talk of 'works of the law'

---

35   Peter T. O'Brien, *The Epistle to the Philippians*, NIGTC (Grand Rapids, MI: Eerdmans, 1991), 379.

36   I stand confident that my own proposals in *NCNU* clarify Paul's use of the phrase.

should not be taken as an attack on self-achievement. (2) There is no hint in Deut. xxvii.26 or in Paul's use of it that the obedience called for is impossible. Deuteronomy certainly did not think so (Deut. xxx.11-14); and neither did Paul (Rom. viii.4). The mistake, once again, has been read into the argument the idea that at this time the law would be satisfied with nothing less than sinlessness, unblemished obedience, that the law was understood as a means to achieving righteousness from scratch. But in Jewish thought to 'abide within all that was written in the law and to do it' meant living within the provisions for sin, through repentance and atonement. That was why Paul was able to describe himself as 'blameless' before his conversion (Phil. iii.6); not because he committed no sin, not because he fulfilled every law without exception, but because the righteousness of the law included use of the sacrificial cult and benefit of the Day of Atonement. That the Judaism, against which Paul here reacts, called for an impossible perfection is not part of the context of the argument at this point and should not be read into it.[37]

While it would be wrong to say that the sacrificial system mitigated sin in its primary function, or even in the strictest sense,[38] the Day of Atonement would meet these ends. Essentially, an Israelite who belonged to the covenant faith, remained in believing-loyalty, and made use of the system of repentance and atonement via the Temple

---

37   James D. G. Dunn, *The Epistle to the Galatians*, BNTC (Peabody, MA: Hendrickson Publishers, 2006), 171.

38   Much of the cult had to do with im/purity, not with sin, and the two ought not be conflated. See Jonathan Klawans, *Impurity and Sin in Ancient Judaism* (Oxford: Oxford University Press, 2000).

cult could be assured of ultimate salvation. Thus the Law does not suppose a legalistic existence as it anticipates and handles sin within its own system. Glossing the OT salvation economy as legalistic is untenable. The thematic threading that lies behind the NT and Paul's letters, therefore, is not the idea of *how* one is saved, but rather *who* is saved.

Judaism and Gentiles

First-century Palestine was a hotbed of religious tension. After nearly a millennium of oppression by outside powers, and now under the thumb of Rome, one notable aspect of the Judaism from which the NT was written was what we may call *ethnocentricism*, or what I like to call *covenantal exclusivity*. This simply means that the Judaism of the first century was a religion of exclusivity. It proudly upheld its identity as God's *unique nation*, but largely abandoned the accompanying call to be a *kingdom of priests* (Exod. 19:5–6). And this sentiment was not entirely misplaced—for the Jews, the nations had long been sources of suffering, oppression, and defilement. Coming on the heels of the Maccabean revolt, this spot remained quite tender in the collective Jewish psyche.

When reading the NT, this prevailing theme must be kept in mind: Judaism at the time functioned as a religious system of exclusivity, viewing anyone not of literal Abrahamic descent as outsiders—the "Other." By and large, being part of the "covenant people" was seen as a guarantee of salvation and status as the elect, a privilege not readily extended to the nations. This belief—that salvation was rooted in national election—is perhaps best illustrated in Matthew 3:9, where John the Immerser says to the Pharisees and Sadducees, "And do not presume to say to yourselves, 'We have Abraham as our father,' for I tell you, God is able from these stones to raise up children for Abraham." As Craig S. Keener writes:

Jewish people commonly believed that they were saved as a people by virtue of their descent from Abraham. The idea of God raising up people from stones would have sounded to John the Baptist's hearers more like pagan mythology (the Greeks had such stories) than reality, but ancients often used the metaphor figuratively. Some scholars have also suggested a wordplay on 'children' and 'stones' in Aramaic; biblical prophets sometimes used puns to hold attention. The God Who could create from dust (Gen 2:7; cf. 1:24) or ribs (2:21) could create from stones; moreover, stones could be used to symbolize God's people (Ex 24:4; 28:9-12; Josh 4:20-21; 1 Kings 18:31). Other prophets had emphasized that God did not need Israel to fulfill His purpose (as in Amos (9.7)."[39]

Gentiles as the "Other" is perhaps best illustrated in Ephesians 2:11–13:

> Therefore remember that at one time you Gentiles in the flesh, called "the uncircumcision" by what is called the circumcision, which is made in the flesh by hands—remember that you were at that time separated from Christ, alienated from the commonwealth of Israel and strangers to the covenants of promise, having no hope and without God in the world. But now in Christ Jesus you who once were far off have been brought near by the blood of Christ.
> —Ephesians 2:11–13

---

39 Craig S. Keener, *The IVP Bible Background Commentary: New Testament* (Downers Grove, IL: IVP Academic, 2014), 52.

The language here colors in the lines of this Jewish exclusivity. For first-century Jews, Gentiles were viewed as being shut out of God's covenant and, in a sense, beyond the reach of salvation. This idea is one of the central themes running through the New Testament—a crucial context often missed by readers, yet necessary for understanding the polemical thrust behind much of its message. As Don B. Garlington put it, "the controversy between Paul and Israel over the law had to do not with 'grace' as opposed to 'legalism' but with ethnic inclusiveness as over against Jewish nationalism."[40]

As we will see in our study of Acts 10, there existed immense Jewish hostility towards Gentiles. For the Second-Temple-Period Jew, the Messiah would come, take center stage, and fulfill the Abrahamic and Davidic covenants, subdue the nations, restore the Land, and usher in a Messianic era of tranquility. It goes without saying that this was not necessarily how God planned to bring about the fullness of the ages. The believing Jew found this unexpected reality to be puzzling, and even the apostles shared this struggle (e.g., Acts 1:6). This nationalistic framework drew support from the prophets, who spoke of God subduing the nations and bringing victory to Israel. This was their hope. And for many, Gentiles simply did not fit into the equation, or not in the way Christ would reveal—as full and equal members of the covenant through faith.

For those who would join the people of Israel, one would have to proselytize, that is, circumcise (if male) and convert formally to Judaism. While scholars like Matthew Thiessen,[41] and more recently

---

40 Don B. Garlington, "The Obedience of Faith": A Pauline Phrase in Historical Context (PhD diss., University of Durham, 1987), abstract.

41 Matthew Thiessen, *Contesting Conversion: Genealogy, Circumcision, and Identity in Ancient Judaism and Christianity* (Oxford: Oxford University Press, 2011); more recently *A Jewish Paul: The Messiah's Herald to the Gentiles* (Grand Rapids, MI: Baker Academic,

Ryan D. Collman,[42] have argued against the validity of circumcising as a means of conversion, noting its original intent for the eighth day, Exodus 12:48 clearly states that a stranger may become circumcised to keep the Passover, and that "he shall be as a native of the land." Yet the verse adds, "But no uncircumcised person shall eat of it," showing that God held to some manner of exclusivity tied to covenant identity, even if only programmatically. The fact that a mixed multitude came out of Egypt with Israel (Exod. 12:38), and that the Davidic lineage includes Gentiles such as Rahab the Jerichoan and Ruth the Moabite (Matt. 1:5), points towards a more universal inclusion of the nations.

Rabbinic literature provides plentiful evidence of Gentiles converting, primarily by way of circumcision and a *mikveh*—a ritual washing that may well be the source domain from which the sacrament of baptism would emerge.[43] In Matthew 23:15, Jesus admonishes the scribes and Pharisees for traveling across sea and land to make a proselyte worse than themselves, and the very term is found throughout the NT denoting converts to Judaism.[44] Michael F. Bird, in writing extensively on the topic, concludes that while Judaism was not a missionary-minded religion per se, it certainly encouraged and welcomed converts to Judaism.[45] As W. D. Davies writes:

2023).

42   Ryan D. Collman, *The Apostle to the Foreskin: Circumcision in the Letters of Paul*, BZAW 259 (Boston: Berlin: De Gruyter, 2023).

43   See the succinct article by Louis J. Feldman, "Conversion to Judaism in Classical Antiquity," *HUCA* 74 (2003), 115–156.

44   Acts 2:11; 6:5; 13:43. For the term *prosēlutos*, see Matthew Thiessen, "Revising the προσήλυτος in 'the LXX,'" *JBL* 132.2 (2013), 333-50; David M. Moffitt and C. Jacob Butera, "P.Duk. inv. 727r: New Evidence for the Meaning and Provenance of the Word προσήλυτος," *JBL* 132.1 (2013), 159-78.

45   Michael F. Bird, *Crossing Over Sea and Land: Jewish Missionary Activity in the Second Temple Period* (Grand Rapids, MI: Baker Academic, 2010).

> With the decline in the belief in the ultimate salvation of
> the Gentiles it came to be recognized that the only hope for
> the latter was to become Jews, i.e. to be naturalized into the
> Jewish people, and it is this that accounts for the considerable
> activity shown in the gaining of proselytes. The New Testa-
> ment supplies evidence for the latter; and the large number of
> proselytes gained shows that Jewish propaganda was success-
> ful.[46]

Shaye J. D. Cohen puts it well: "acceptance of circumcision is the acceptance of Judaism."[47] What emerges before us is a picture that would have massive social and religious implications: unless one was to formally convert to Judaism, they could not really know the God of Israel. An issue from a social perspective was the view of circumcision as barbaric in the Greco-Roman world,[48] but the real issue was that of exclusivity. That Gentiles would be forced to circumcise into Judaism both implies that faith is not enough, which explains the severity of Paul's language on the topic, and also assumes that there is a funda- mental problem with a Gentile, reinforcing their status as "Other." Paul, in contrast, would loudly proclaim "For neither circumcision nor uncircumcision is of any efficacy, but rather a new creation" (Gal. 6:15, my translation).

This is all to say that the NT is often preoccupied with defending the validity of Gentiles becoming members of God's people without the need to "become Jews." Decades ago, Krister Stendahl challenged

---

46   W. D. Davies, *Paul and Rabbinic Judaism: Some Rabbinic Elements in Pauline Theology* (Minneapolis: Fortress Press, 1980), 63.

47   Shaye J. D. Cohen, "Crossing the Boundary and Becoming a Jew," *HTR* 82.1 (1989), 27.

48   Troy W. Martin, "Paul and Circumcision," in *Paul in the Greco-Roman World: A Handbook*, Vol. 1, ed. J. Paul Sampley (New York: T&T Clark, 2016), 113–142.

the Church to read Paul's justification language within such a theme, urging readers to understand that the issue Paul was faced with was not one of legalism but, rather, one of Gentiles being admitted as full members to God's People in Christ.[49] This, for example, was the purpose behind the Council of Jerusalem (cf. Acts 15:1, 5) and the central message of Peter's vision in Acts 10: God has gloriously called in the nations along with restored Israel. This revelation and fact needed to be defended—even to Jesus's often stuck-in-their-ways disciples, and to their fellow (sometimes nefarious) countrymen.

Rather than us finding an ethics issue, we are typically dealing with an ethnics one, and this holds true for Peter's vision. While we must evaluate each and every passage based on their own unique context, this is the prevailing theme behind most of the NT. Legalistic and uninformed readings unduly slant pericopes, while a proper exegetical approach allows us to read what is actually going on in any given situation.

Jesus's View of the Law

Given the highly polemical and charged nature of many of the epistles, reading Paul and the other apostles involves navigating a complex and often ambiguous environment—one that deals with issues extending beyond an inner-Jewish debate. Compared to the Gospels, the letters are less reliable for evaluating the role of the Law in early Christianity. Additionally, these later writings incorporate a milieu of literary elements—such as Greco-Roman cultural references, new linguistic expressions and devices, various allegories, rhetorical strategies, and other argumentative nuances—that further complicate

---

49   Krister Stendahl, "The Apostle Paul and the Introspective Conscience of the West," *HTR* 56.3 (1963), 199–215.

interpretation. In contrast, the Gospels present both the direct words of Jesus and a more straightforward setting in which the Law was part of everyday life. In other words, while passages in, say, Paul's letters (which Peter warns are difficult to understand; 2 Pet. 3:15–16) may be ambiguous, such confusion is less likely in the Gospels. Jesus's own words and actions clear up any confusion regarding the Law and serve as the measuring stick by which the rest of the NT should be evaluated.

So, what was Jesus's view of the Law? Based on his actions throughout the Gospel accounts, we find no instance of Jesus disregarding the Law; rather, he upholds it to its fullest standard.[50] And judging by his words, we see that he fully affirmed the Law in no uncertain terms. In Matthew 5:17 we read, "Do not think that I have come to abolish the Law or the Prophets; I have not come to abolish them but to fulfill them." David Wilber has very recently published a treatment exclusively on Jesus's words in Matthew 5:17–20, and he has argued persuasively against the common antinomian view—a view that is

---

[50] One potential objection to this point arises from the conflict with the Pharisees over plucking grain on the Sabbath, where Jesus calls himself "Lord of the Sabbath" and says that the Sabbath was "made for man" (Mark 2:23–28). However, Jesus and his disciples were actually fully in compliance with the Law. There is no prohibition in the Law against eating or preparing food on the Sabbath, nor can the act of "plucking" (*tillō*) heads of grain (*stachus*) and "rubbing them with the hands" (*psōchontes tais chersi*, Luke 6:1) reasonably be equated with gathering, as in the case of the manna prohibition in Exodus 16:22–30. What Jesus and his disciples were doing—walking through a field and taking what they needed to eat—is explicitly permitted in Deuteronomy 23:25. Given that they were hungry and in need, Jesus's actions in this context were neither a violation of the Law nor a dismissal of the Sabbath. For more on this, see John R. Van Maaren, *The Gospel of Mark within Judaism: Reading the Second Gospel in its Ethnic Landscape* (PhD diss., McMaster University, 2019), 303–304; David Wilber, *Remember the Sabbath: What the New Testament Says About Sabbath Observance for Christians* (Clover, SC: Pronomian Publishing, 2022).

quickly losing favor within the scholarly world. The antinomian view holds that Jesus coming to "fulfill" (*plērōsai*) the Law means that he kept the Law so that we do not have to.[51] But given the content of the six antitheses (Matt 5:21–43) and the verses that immediately follow, including Jesus's admonition to his followers to "do" and "teach" the commandments (Matt. 5:19), interpreting Matthew 5:17 as a salvation-historical claim ignores the true nature and context of Jesus's statement. The problem with the view that Jesus fulfilled the Law so that it is no longer relevant is that, no matter how you spin it, the Law gets abolished. As Wilber comments, "The biggest problem with this idea is that it sounds exactly like what Jesus said he did not come to do. There is no difference between abolishing something and making it obsolete; the result is the same. And since Jesus contrasts 'fulfill' (πληρόω) with 'abolish' (καταλύω), these words cannot mean the same thing."[52] Wilber persuasively argues that Jesus did not come to *abolish* the Law but rather to properly interpret the Law. He comments that interpreters who hold to the antinomian view often approach passages like Matthew 5:18 "with a predetermined conclusion about what the

---

51 This argument is often based on Jesus's inclusion of the phrase "or the Prophets." As Robert Banks notes, this addition was likely made by Matthew due to his "general interest in the fulfillment of prophecy," though he adds that "a non-theological motive is at work and that more often than not it is merely an unconscious association of ideas that lies behind its assertion…the addition of *hoi prophētai*, therefore, does not spring from a desire to introduce a reference to Christ's fulfillment of OT prophecy, but is rather a simple expansion resulting from an association of two frequently combined ideas." The focus of the formula, contrary to common suggestion, is on the Law rather than the Prophets: "the exclusive concentration upon the Law in the following verses (vss. 18–19) strengthens this suggestion" (Robert Banks, "Matthew's Understanding of the Law: Authenticity and Interpretation in Matthew 5:17–20," *JBL* 93.2 [1974], 228).

52 David Wilber, *How Jesus Fulfilled the Law: A Pronomian Pocket Guide to Matthew 5:17–20* (Clover, SC: Pronomian Publishing, 2024), 15.

text is allowed to say" and fail to take into account the very plainness of the text.[53] Ultimately, Jesus upholds the Law and calls his followers to exceed that of the Pharisees' righteousness (v. 20), calling us unto even greater holiness than just what the Law calls for.[54]

Mark 7 and Jesus's Declaring All Foods Clean

A brief mention of Mark 7 is necessary for our purposes, as it serves as the seedbed for the idea that the food laws were abrogated. While a full treatment of this pericope is beyond our current scope, a few key details must be noted.[55] The situation begins with the Pharisees questioning Jesus about why his disciples eat "with hands that we defiled [*koinais*], that is, unwashed" (Mark 7:2). Mark then adds a parenthetical comment: "For the Pharisees and all the Jews do not eat unless they wash their hands properly, holding to the tradition of the elders" (Mark 7:3).[56] This comment sets the context for the entire dispute—Jesus is addressing the (pre-Mishnaic?) traditions, often

---

53   Wilber, *How Jesus Fulfilled the Law*, 23. See also Ulrich Luz: "the attempt to interpret v. 18d christologically to mean that in Christ's death and resurrection 'everything' predicted in the OT has 'happened'…would require complicated eisegesis of the text" (*Matthew 1–7*, Hermenia [Augsburg: Fortress Press, 2007], 219).

54   I cover the six antitheses, demonstrating their meaning and what Jesus is doing with the Law, in "Appendix One: To 'Fulfill' the Law: Matthew 5.17–7.12" in *NCNU*, 772–801.

55   I cover Mark 7:1–23 and its relevant context quite extensively in *Purity, Politics, and Parables: A Narratological and Exegetical Study on the Handwashing Conflict in Mark 7:1–23* (Independent, 2025).

56   The practice is well attested in tannaitic literature—in the Mishnah there is an entire tractate titled *Yadayim* (lit, "hands") on the general practice; see also T. *Eruvin* 21b; T. *Shabbat* 13b–15a; Tosefta *Berakhot* 63, and archaeological evidence of washing basins. See, for instance, Thomas Kazen, *Issues of Impurity in Early Judaism*, Itero 4 (Stockholm: Enskila Högskolan Stockholm, 2021), 113–135.

referred to as the "oral law," rather than the written commandments of the Torah.

As we discussed above, Jesus quotes Isaiah 29:13 (Mark 7:6–7), condemns the Pharisees' practices like Qorban as being a violation of the Word of God (Mark 7:9–13),[57] and turns to the crowd and says, "There is nothing outside a person that by going into him can defile him, but the things that come out of a person are what defile him" (Mark 7:15). After leaving, the disciples ask him privately about this parable, to which he repeats his statement and adds that "it enters not his heart but is stomach, and is expelled," with most translations then adding another parenthetical comment, "(Thus he declared all foods clean)" (Mark 7:19). While verse 15 is its own enigma, it is verse 19c's *katharizōn panta ta brōmata* ("cleansing all the food") that is used to suggest that Jesus declared all foods clean.

The scholarship on Mark 7:1–23 is abundant, but in recent years the antinomian view has faced significant challenges by some.[58] The

---

57   For the larger background information on the practice, and abuses of it, see Benjamin D. Gordon, *Land and Temple: Field Sacralization and the Agrarian Priesthood of Second Temple Judaism*, SJ 87 (Berlin: Boston: De Gruyter, 2020).

58   Besides those cited below, see Roger P. Booth, *Jesus and the Laws of Purity: Tradition History and Legal History in Mark 7*, JSNTSup 13 (Sheffield: Sheffield Academic Press, 1986); Ian H. Henderson, Jesus, *Rhetoric and Law*, BIS 20 (Leiden: Brill, 1996), 383–387; James G. Crossley, *The Date of Mark's Gospel: Insight from the Law in Earliest Christianity*, JSNTSup 266 (New York: T&T Clark, 2004), 183–202; Daniel Boyarin, *The Jewish Gospels: The Story of the Jewish Christ* (New York: The New Press, 2012), 103–128; J. Andrew Doole, *What was Mark for Matthew? An Examination of Matthew's Relationship and Attitude to His Primacy Source*, WUNT 344 (Tübingen: Mohr Siebeck, 2013), 86; M. John-Patrick O'Connor, *The Moral Life According to Mark*, LNTS 667 (New York: T&T Clark, 2022), 126–128; J. A. Lloyd, *Archaeology and the Itinerant Jesus: A Historical Enquiry into Jesus' Itinerant Ministry in the North*, WUNT 564 (Tübingen: Mohr Siebeck, 2022), 334; Steven James Stiles, *Jesus' Fulfillment of the Torah and Prophets: Inherited Strategies and Torah Interpretation in Matthew's Gospel*, WUNT 594 (Tübingen: Mohr

antinomian reading of Mark 7:19 stands as a quintessence of eisegesis, as it conflicts with the overall context of the pericope itself as well as Matthew's almost parallel account: "But to eat with unwashed hands does not defile anyone" (Matt. 15:20). Here we find one of the very few occasions where an easily misunderstood passage is directly and unambiguously explained by another biblical author. Yet, scholars and readers alike often neglect Matthew's clarification, choosing instead to uphold their traditional interpretations of Mark 7:19.

The irony here is that this is essentially what the Pharisees were doing: rejecting the Law to uphold their own traditions, which, to be sure, were false interpretations and impositions upon the Bible. Here more irony is spelled out in that if Jesus rebukes these Pharisees for abandoning the Law for the sake of their traditions, how are we to justify him abrogating the Law himself? That would make him contradictory at best and a hypocrite at worst. Moreover, the antinomian argument suffers immense difficulty in that if the Law was abrogated on account of Jesus's death on the cross, how and why is Jesus abrogating the Law in Mark 7:19, years prior to Calvary? Such an argument crumbles by its very own framework. Finally, as we will see when we examine Peter's vision, if Jesus indeed cleansed all foods back in Mark 7:19, did the apostle miss the memo (Acts 10:14)?

Understanding the situation within the realm of Jewish *halakha* (interpretation) is crucial, as Jesus's proclamations in Mark 7:15 and 19 do not deviate from the Law. First, while there were causes of impurity detailed in passages like Leviticus 12 and 15, *unclean animals*

Siebeck, 2023); 148–154. To date, Thomas Kazen's various works remain perhaps the most thorough treatments on the topic. However, Eike Arend Mueller's unpublished 2015 Andrews University PhD diss., *Cleansing the Common: A Narrative-Intertextual Study of Mark 7:1–23*, though unfortunately neglected, is likely the most thorough and persuasive treatment to date.

would not defile someone: they were prohibited but not defiling.[59] Since the discussion between Jesus and the Pharisees in Mark 7 centers on issues of "purity" and "defilement," the focus of the passage cannot be on unclean animals. Second, Jesus's declaration of what is outside a person not defiling them is biblically correct, since what defiled people came from within—such as a bodily discharge, death emanating from a corpse, blood, etc.[60] Third, Jesus's position on moral impurity is attested in Jewish literature and would be a thoroughly *halakhic* pronouncement on his part.[61] Fourth, the entire focus of the pericope is on Jewish tradition and not the Law—extending interpretive implications beyond this realm is extracting more from the situation than is present.

Since a full overview of Mark 7 is beyond the scope of the present study, I recommend Logan Williams's recently published article that persuasively argues against the antinomian view. In his article, Williams argues that since "the comments about immersion, cleansing cups, and washing hands in 7:2–5 are practices related to the domain of *tohorah* [purities], not *kashrut* [food laws]," and because the Pharisees and scribes are challenging the disciples not over what is lawful (*exestin*), but over their traditions, Jesus's response is confined strictly

59 Yair Furstenberg, "Defilement Penetrating the Body: A New Understanding of Contamination in Mark 7:15," NTS 54 (2008), 176–200; John van Maaren, "Does Mark's Jesus Abrogate the Torah? Jesus' Purity Logion and Its Illustration in Mark 7:15–23," JJMJS 4 (2017), 21–41.

60 Daniel Boyarin, "An Isogloss in First-Century Jewry: Josephus and Mark on the Purpose of the Law" in *The Faces of Torah: Studies in the Texts and Contexts of Ancient Judaism in Honor of Steven Fraade*, ed. Michal Bar-Asher Siegal, Tzvi Novick, and Christine Hayes (Göttingen: V&R Academic, 2017), 63–81.

61 See esp. Jesper Svartvik, *Mark and Mission: Mk 7:1 – 23 in its Narrative and Historical Contexts*, CBNTS 32 (Stockholm: Almqvist & Wiksell, 2000), 372–406.

to this realm of ritual purity.[62] The distinctiveness of Williams's proposal lies in his grammatical argument, where he offers a translation similar to that of the KJV.[63] This approach accomplishes two things: first, it avoids the awkwardness of attaching *katharizōn* ("purify," "cleanse") to the main verb *legei* ("said") that appears about thirty-six words earlier. Instead, Williams identifies *anthrōpos* ("man") as the subject.[64] Second, it aligns with Greco-Roman anatomical views that the stomach purifies food, as well as the Jewish understanding that excrement—the final destination of digested food—was not considered a source of defilement.[65] In sum, he explains that this reading implies "ritually defiled food cannot defile humans through ingestion because humans purify all foods from ritual impurity through digestion."[66] This statement essentially captures the entire dispute in Mark 7, which was about whether unwashed hands handling potentially impure food can cause defilement.

While Williams's proposals are still in the reception stage, they are not necessarily new, and his work adds a compelling contribution to the growing scholarly view that interpreting Mark 7:19 as abrogating the food laws is untenable. Ultimately, when considering the parallel in Matthew and the clear context of ritual purity and Jewish tradition, the idea that Jesus is abrogating the Law (and doing so hypocriti-

---

62   Logan A. Williams, "The Stomach Purifies All Foods: Jesus' Anatomical Argument in Mark 7.18–19," *NTS* 70 (2024), 375.

63   "Because it entereth not into his heart, but into the belly, and goeth out into the draught, purging all meats."

64   Williams, "The Stomach Purifies," 379–383. Williams shows that similar constructions appear in Isaiah 28:5–6 and Psalm 103:13–14 LXX.

65   Williams, "The Stomach Purifies," 385–389.

66   Williams, "The Stomach Purifies," 384.

cally) appears to be more a matter of interpretive tradition than sound exegesis.[67]

Setting the Table

This chapter has aimed to resituate our understanding within the first-century context. The main takeaway is this: the Judaism of Jesus's day was not a legalistic, works-based system of salvation, but rather a religion of covenantal exclusivity—viewing those outside Abrahamic descent as separate from God's unique people. As a result, Gentiles were expected either to convert to Judaism or remain without God in the world. Yet the OT anticipated a time when the Messiah would come to gather both Israel *and* those of the nations who seek the Lord, reconciling all things—and all people—to God. This eschatological and apocalyptic worldview underlies much of the NT, which assumes and announces its fulfillment. The historical ethnic divide between Jew and Gentile—God's holy and clean people versus the common and unclean nations—is also a theme that runs just beneath the surface of much of the NT, standing in tension with the eschatological expectations proclaimed by Israel's prophets. With this in mind, we

---

67   In *Purity, Politics, and Parables* I investigate Williams's proposals in more detail and ultimately argue, instead, for a parenthetical (editorial) comment—specifically an anacoluthic participial phrase in Mark 7:19c. I choose to translate *katharizōn panta ta brōmata* as, "In saying this, he thus decreed all of the foods clean," with a significantly stronger and more reliable grammatical and syntactical argument. The significant difference is that in 7:15 and 19 Jesus actually upholds the Levitical principles of impurity and its transfer via what I call *parabolic halakha*. He uses the biblical understanding of impurity transmission to rebut the Pharisees' false understanding of it, which is what stands behind the hand washing practice in the first place. Nothing in the account suggests that he is doing anything other than providing *halakhic* ("teaching-interpretation-walking") instruction on the issue at hand, i.e., the (nonexistent) contamination of clean (*kosher*) foods.

are now prepared to approach Peter's vision within its proper religious and historical context.

CHAPTER 2
THE VISION IN ACTS 10

Immediately following the Gospels is the book we call the *Acts of the Apostles*. There is much significance in this title that is often overlooked. Luke opens the book by writing, "In the first book, O Theophilus, I have dealt with all that Jesus began to do and teach, until the day when he was taken up, after he had given commands through the Holy Spirit to the apostles whom he had chosen" (Acts 1:1). Acts, then, documents the "passing of the baton" from Jesus to the apostles, who were commissioned to carry forward the Gospel. The truth cemented in Jesus's words and actions is now entrusted to those he appointed.[1] As Eckhard Schnabel writes, "while the first volume

---

1   Jesus's teachings continuing in apostolic authority is demonstrated throughout the NT, as we will discuss below. A notable example comes by way of the phrase "the teaching of Christ" in 2 John. Colin G. Kruse, following E. R. Wendland, writes that "the 'teaching of Christ' (*didachē tou Christou*) could be construed as either a subjective genitive ('what Christ taught') or an objective genitive ('teaching about Christ'), but [Wendland] suggests that this is another example of what he calls semantic density, where the author intended both meanings to be picked up by the readers. That is, it was important not only to confess that Jesus Christ had come in the flesh (teaching about Christ) but also to acknowledge and obey Christ's teaching/command to love one another" (*The Letters of John*, PNTC [Grand Rapids, MI: Eerdmans, 2020], 227. Kruse cites E. R. Wendland, "'What is Truth:' Semantic Density and the Language of the Johannine Epistles (with Special Reference to 2 John)," *NeoT* 24.2 [1990], 310). In 2 John both the commandments of Jesus and the Incarnation are in view of this "teaching," so that apostolic proclamation can be seen as authoritative (equal to "the teaching of Christ") seems proper. Karen H. Jobes remarks that "it cannot be strictly limited to the teaching of Jesus during his earthly life, for Jesus himself promised that his apostles would receive further instruction from the Spirit after his death…Teaching given by Jesus becomes teaching about Christ" (*1, 2, and 3 John*, ZECNT [Grand Rapids, MI: Zondervan Academic, 2014], 270). I would add that apostolic teachings are considered like Christ's, since they write under the

[the Gospel of Luke] described what Jesus began to do and teach, the second volume describes what Jesus continues to do and to teach in and through the ministry of the apostles."[2] Understanding Acts as the record of the Gospel now going forth through the apostles and into the nations is crucial, especially considering Luke's deliberate use of thematic and structural literary techniques. Much of his material must be read with this larger context in mind. As Schnabel further notes, the predominant themes in Acts are "the identity of the church as God's people, and the mission of the church as witnesses of Jesus."[3]

It is this larger theme which guides our investigation here. As Acts relays the emergence of a new church—a new people of God characterized not by Israelite descent but by placing faith in Jesus—the topic of the Law will be not only of immense importance, but its relationship to the Church, and especially Gentile believers, will be defined by the accounts we read. A certain reverence must be given to what we find in the book of the apostles' ministries and developments in doctrine, and their instructions must be seen as universally binding. Such a theme is found in Matthew 16:18–19 where Jesus says to Peter, "And I tell you, you are Peter, and on this rock I will build My church, and the gates of hell shall not prevail against it. I will give you the keys of the kingdom of heaven, and whatever you bind on earth shall be bound in heaven, and whatever you loose on earth shall be loosed in heaven." Two common misunderstandings surround this passage. The first is the idea that Peter is given the keys to heaven, which somehow results in him standing at the pearly gates, granting souls admission—a familiar image to many,

---

inspiration of the Spirit and would have their experience with him to remember.

2   Eckhart Schnabel, *Acts*, ZECNT 5 (Grand Rapids, MI: Zondervan Academic, 2012), 102.

3   Schnabel, *Acts*, 48.

though incorrect.[4] The second misconception is messier: that Peter, and by extension the Church, is being granted authority over demons. This view is especially common in charismatic circles, where believers claim to "bind" Satan or "loosen" demonic strongholds in their lives (e.g., "I bind you, Satan," or "I loosen every demonic oppression, on earth and in heaven"). While such practices may be supported by other passages, they are not the correct interpretation of Jesus's words to Peter in this context.

In Matthew 16:18–19, the words for "binding" and "loosing," or rather "tying" and "untying," are to be understood as administrative authority. As France writes, "The terms are used in rabbinic literature for declaring what is and is not permitted."[5] This authority is extended to all of the disciples, not exclusively to Peter, though he yet remains "the first among equals."[6] This fact is significant for us, as what we will encounter in Acts may involve a complete reevaluation of the Law in terms of its practical application, along with authoritative decisions that continue to carry weight today. While each of these instances—if and when we find them—must first be evaluated based on their immediate context, the authority of the apostles must also be acknowledged. Reflecting on Jesus's commissioning of Peter, Matthias Konradt spells out some of the obvious implications:

---

4   See R. T. France: "The traditional portrayal of Peter as porter at the pearly gates depends on misunderstanding 'the kingdom of heaven' here as a designation of the afterlife rather than denoting God's rule among his people on earth" (*The Gospel of Matthew*, NICNT [Grand Rapids, MI: Eerdmans, 2007], 449). See also his comments on this passage drawing from Isaiah 22:20–22.

5   France, *Matthew*, 449.

6   France, *Matthew*, 449.

Speaking of handing over the keys to the kingdom thus has in view that Peter is here being entrusted with authentic transmission of Jesus' interpretation of the Law and his ethical instruction, in order to open to people the possibility of entering the kingdom of heaven. In the overall context of Matthew, v. 19 is to be read and nuanced in relation to 23:13: Jesus pronounces woes on the scribes and Pharisees because of their false teaching, in which God's will is obscured by human doctrines, and which closes people off from entering the kingdom of heaven (15:3–9). The statement in 16:19 forms the positive counterpart to 23:13 and by this contrast formulates the claim of the church to be the true guardian of the theological traditions of Israel. This stands alongside the directly preceding context, in which the disciples were warned about the teaching of the Pharisees and Sadducees (16:5–12).[7]

Konradt helpfully contributes further insight into the specific meaning of binding and loosing:

The metaphor of the keys of the kingdom of heaven is developed by the pair of terms 'bind' and 'loose,' which in the light of rabbinic usage, are to be understood in the sense of 'forbid' and 'permit' (e.g., m. Ter. 5.4; m. Pesah 4.5; 6.2), and in fact refer to the interpretation of the Torah. The declaration in 18:18 will show that this includes the authority to exercise church discipline or to forgive transgressions (cf. John 20:23; as well as Josephus, *War* 1.111, in reference to

---

7   Matthias Konradt, *The Gospel According to Matthew: A Commentary*, translated by M. Eugene Boring (Waco, TX: Baylor University Press, 2020), 254.

the judicial responsibility of imprisonment or acquittal). In 16:19, however, the emphasis is placed primarily on teaching, as suggested by the metaphor of the keys to the kingdom of heaven. Peter's authority to bind and loose thus refers to the task of ensuring that the Torah developed in the teaching of Jesus (cf. esp. 5:17–48) is faithfully handed down as the basic standard and made fruitful as the church's point of orientation in the concrete ethical challenges it faces. An interpretation of the Law or instruction on ethical action based on Jesus' teaching (see 28:20a) has the assurance that what is decided on earth is also validated by God.[8]

What we see here is that apostolic authority, by the authority given directly from Jesus the Lawmaker himself, covers all areas of doctrine and instruction, but most importantly for our purposes, the proper interpretation and application of the Law. In the last chapter we pointed out that the way Jesus viewed, entreated, and spoke about the Law is the same way we must as well. Equally, however, we must understand that if we find what we feel to be contradictory interpretations of/over the Law and its application in later apostolic writings, we must concede the fact that apostolic authority overrides *our* interpretations. This applies to both sides of the aisle. The apostles make a plethora of decisions with theological and ethical implications in Acts. By lot and prayer they choose Matthias to replace Judas as one of the twelve apostles (Acts 1:12–26) and men to execute the distribution of church funds (Acts 6:1–6), showing ecclesial functioning. With the Spirit they make decisions regarding Gentile inclusion within the church (Acts 10), decisions over what is required of Gentiles (Acts 15), and even give

---

8   Konradt, *Matthew*, 254–255.

authoritative instruction to one another (Acts 21). Additionally, Jesus continues to teach and reveal things to his apostles through visions, dreams, direct teaching, and the Spirit.

In order to be objective, one must accept the *possibility* that Jesus could, *if* it were God's original intent, "overturn" the Law's applicability, especially considering the incoming of Gentiles. It is *possible* that he chose to reveal this plan only after (a) his Ascension and even (b) the appointed time for the Gentiles to accept the Gospel, primarily governed under apostolic authority and revelation. This observation highlights the importance of reading the NT in its proper context: how we handle the immediate context can sway the material at hand, and the larger discussion, in either direction. It is my contention, however, that a proper reading grounded in the context only validates Jesus's high view of the Law. Part of what we have begun to understand and apply is the pericope's context and theology within Luke's narrative, which centers on the ushering in of God's universal plan of salvation—the creation of a new people in his Son—and sets the tenor of Luke's tune.

Introduction to the Birth of the Church

When did the Church begin? Was it at the start of Jesus's ministry? At the Cross? Or sometime later? While this is an important historical question, it is even more so a theological one: when did what we now understand as "the Church" truly begin, and can we assign a specific date or event to its origin? Rather than pinpointing a single moment, it may be more accurate to view the birth of the Church as an era, with its own timeline of sorts, that gradually developed into a unified body made up of both Jew and Gentile. This, in fact, is the central concern of much of the NT. In Acts, Luke seems keenly aware of the importance of this larger motif, which is set against the backdrop of prophetic expectations regarding the restoration of Israel and the ingathering of the nations.[9] Paul will carry this theme forward as well, but it must be stressed here in order to read the passages discussed in the following sections within their larger context—within their symbolic and interpretive world that Luke employs. Put another way, Luke presents a narrative with an overarching theme, and the events and situations he describes are set within—and made clearer by—that larger theological vision. While we've already addressed some of Luke's broader themes, here we will focus on three key "mini-themes" found within his theological biography: the creation of a covenant nation, the gradual inclusion of the nations, and the turning of the gospel primarily toward the Gentiles. These themes form the ground of Luke's narrative.

The Creation of a Nation

Luke does not begin Acts without first mentioning events involving Jesus. Up until Acts 1:11, Jesus is still present with the disciples, and Luke records his Ascension. In Acts 1:5, Jesus tells the disciples that they will soon be baptized with the Holy Spirit. In response, they ask, "Lord, will You at this time restore the kingdom to Israel?" (Acts

---

9   On Luke's presentation and acute awareness of this motif, see Michael E. Fuller, *The Restoration of Israel: Israel's Re-Gathering and the Fate of the Nations in Early Jewish Literature and Luke-Acts*, BZW 138 (Boston: Berlin: De Gruyter, 2006); James Meek, *The Gentile Mission in Old Testament Citations in Acts: Text, Hermeneutic, and Purpose*, LNTS 385 (Edinburgh: T&T Clark, 2008); David Pao, *Acts and the Isaianic New Exodus* (Eugene, OR: Wipf & Stock, 2016); Arco den Hejier, *Portraits of Paul's Performance in the Book of Acts: Luke's Apologetic Strategy in the Depiction of Paul as a Messenger of God*, WUNT 2/556 (Tübingen: Mohr Siebeck, 2021); Isaac W. Oliver, *Luke's Jewish Eschatology: The National Restoration of Israel in Luke-Acts* (Oxford: Oxford University Press, 2021). For a view with the Spirit in focus, see Max Turner, *Power From on High: The Spirit in Israel's Restoration and Witness in Luke-Acts* (Eugene, OR: Wipf & Stock, 2015).

1:6). Jesus responds that it is not for them to know the times or seasons (Acts 1:7) but that they will receive power when the Holy Spirit comes upon them, and that they will be his witnesses "in Jerusalem and in all Judea and Samaria, and to the end of the earth" (Acts 1:8). This moment reveals that the disciples were still holding onto the common Messianic expectations of their day[10] and had not yet fully understood what Jesus was truly doing. Their confusion is understandable, given the often ambiguous nature of prophetic fulfillment since the Incarnation. However, rather than affirming their expectations of a restored earthly kingdom, Jesus redirects their focus to the coming of the Spirit and their mission as his witnesses to the four corners of the earth.

In the next chapter, we read that "the day of Pentecost arrived, and they were all together in one place" (Acts 2:1), and that the Holy Spirit came upon them like a mighty rushing wind, filling them and enabling them to "speak in other tongues as the Spirit gave them utterance" (Acts 2:4). This was the fulfillment of the promised Holy Spirit. However, this event loses its significance if we don't read it against its OT background—namely, its connection to the feast of Pentecost, or Shavuot. Luke provides a wealth of narratological clues to highlight this connection. As he records the disciples speaking in "other tongues" through the Holy Spirit, he writes the following:

> Now there were dwelling in Jerusalem Jews, devout men from
> every nation under heaven. And at this sound the multitude
> came together, and they were bewildered, because each one

---

10   By this I mean that the disciples still held on to the Jewish nationalistic idea of Jesus
      throwing down the nations (in particular, Rome), in line with Jewish expectations, but
      clearly not in line with the unfolding plan of God, which would soon be revealed as not
      coming as Israel exactly expected.

was hearing them speak in his own language. And they were amazed and astonished, saying, "Are not all these who are speaking Galileans? And how is it that we hear, each of us in his own native language? Parthians and Medes and Elamites and residents of Mesopotamia, Judea and Cappadocia, Pontus and Asia, Phrygia and Pamphylia, Egypt and the parts of Libya belonging to Cyrene, and visitors from Rome, both Jews and proselytes, Cretans and Arabians—we hear them telling in our own tongues the mighty works of God."
—Acts 2:6–11

The listing of these nations seems purposeful. Some of these foreigners mocked the disciples, saying that they were drunk (Acts 2:13), to which Peter stands up and preaches, saying, "this is what was uttered through the prophet Joel: 'And in the last days it shall be, God declares, that I will pour out My Spirit on all flesh, and your sons and daughters shall prophesy, and your young men shall see visions, and your old men shall dream dreams" (Acts 2:16–17). The prophecy here is Joel 2:28–31 and relates to the eschatological age where God's Spirit would be poured out upon the end-times remnant. Whatever had just occurred before these men of many nations, Peter contextualizes it as fulfilled prophecy, and specifically fulfilled prophecy pertaining to the eschatological age.

Though fragmented, the allusion to Pentecost here most likely points back to the event at Sinai, where (a) God descended upon the mountain with wind, fire, and noise, and (b) Israel entered into covenant with God. Richard I. Pervo, for example, writes, "The signs accompanying the revelation are those of the classic HB [Hebrew Bible] epiphany: wind, fire, and noise, of which the Sinai theophany (Exod. 19:16–19) is a prime example. There are many others, but Sinai deserves priority because it is a foundational epiphany. The readers of Acts need not have known this specific intertextual link nor the proposed liturgical connection,"[11] suggesting that Luke does not need to make an explicit reference to Sinai, nor rely on a commonly known Jewish association between the two events. Though the Sinai-Pentecost connection is implicitly made in interpretive tradition, it remains quite glaring. Sejin Park, in *Pentecost and Sinai*, clearly illustrates the strong parallels between the two.[12] We should follow that line of interpretation, recognizing that the giving of the Spirit signifies both the presence of God and the recurring biblical motif of making a people for himself.

Pervo also sees the story of Babel here with foreigners listed[13] and sees the event "revealed as both an eschatological event of new creation and a utopian restoration of the unity of the human race. In this thrilling narrative Luke expresses fundamental theological principles: the

---

11   Richard I. Pervo, *Acts: A Commentary* (Augsburg: Fortress Press, 2008), 61.

12   Sejin Park, *Pentecost and Sinai: The Festival of Weeks as a Celebration of the Sinai Event*, LHBOTS 342 (Edinburgh: T&T Clark, 2008). Park examines traditions of Sinai and Pentecost within the theme of covenant renewal in Jubilees (78–127) and Qumran literature (128–175) against the theme in Luke-Acts (176–238). Though he concludes that "by the rabbinic period, the Festival of Weeks was strongly associated with the giving of the Law and was celebrated in commemoration of this momentous event" (239), the lack of any explicit dates given cloud any firm conclusion. Nevertheless, "the groundwork for such an association is already in place" (241), and he demonstrates that due to the (albeit somewhat vague) dating, Pentecost exists as the most likely holiday for the Sinai event. Jubilees makes an explicit connection, followed by the community at Qumran. Park also sees the theophany of Acts 2 being similar to that of the Sinai event, and especially Philo's description of it. Helpful to these points are Michael LeFabvre's investigations in *The Liturgy of Creation: Understanding Calendars in Old Testament Context* (Downers Grove, IL: IVP Academic, 2019). Despite the ambiguity of the text, it would seem reasonable to assume a Shavuot-Pentecost date for Sinai, at least in tradition.

13   Which represents the Diaspora more than a typical connection to the Table of Nations, it could be argued.

---

gift of the Spirit is the present eschatological benefit, and this gift is for the entire human race."[14] G. K. Beale enhances such views and draws out the symbolic and allegorical nuances of the text particularly in the use of temple language,[15] furthering our interpretation that in Acts 2 we have a fulfillment of what Sinai typified, the eschatological gift of the Spirit, as a theophany, both making a nation and the ingathering of all of the nations, reversing the event at Babel. The nations present and the Spirit's descent illustrate to us that the new, eschatological people of God—the newly constituted nation in Christ—had been made, marked by the giving of the Spirit. For our purposes, this is a detail unable to be missed and is inseparable from both the literary context of the chapter and Acts, as well as the theological context and flow of the Bible's grand story as a whole.

Compounding Expansion to the Nations

Throughout Acts, we see a thematic and compounding expansion of the Gospel to the nations through various groups, following a pattern that echoes Israel's own experience at Pentecost. After the stoning of Stephen in chapter 7 and the mention of Paul persecuting the church (Acts 8:1–3), we read of Philip preaching the Gospel in Samaria, where many come to believe (Acts 8:4–13). The Samaritans were essentially "half-Jews" and had quite an uneasy relationship with the Jews (cf. John 4), making this a significant development in terms of who could now receive the Gospel. A thematic clue is that the apostles had to come and pray for the Samaritans to receive the Holy Spirit (Acts 8:14–16), suggesting that the Spirit was beginning to open the

---

14   Pervo, *Acts*, 61–62.

15   G. K. Beale, "The Descent of the Eschatological Temple in the Form of the Spirit at Pentecost," 2 parts, *Tyndale Bulletin* 56, no. 1 (2005): 73–102; 56, no. 2 (2005): 63–90.

promise of the Gospel to all nations. Chapter 8 ends with the account of Philip and the Ethiopian eunuch, who believes and is baptized. This man was likely a proselyte or at least a God-fearer, and he was clearly a Gentile. The fact that he was a eunuch may hold further significance: he would have been physically unable to undergo circumcision for conversion to Judaism. Yet, the new way into God's people had now been opened by way of baptism and faith. The true significance lies in the fact that a Gentile had now received the Gospel—this new faith was not limited to the Jewish people, but extended to all who would receive it.

Acts 9 opens with the conversion of Paul, the apostle to the Gentiles. The narrative then shifts to Peter, who travels to Joppa, performs miracles, and remains there (Acts 9:43). Many readers overlook an important detail: Joppa is the same city Jonah fled to when he refused to go to Nineveh—the mortal enemy of Israel and a city filled with Gentiles. Nineveh was a Gentile city par excellence, if you will, and Jonah's attempt to escape to Tarshish, Spain,[16] represented perhaps a flight to the furthest place one could go. The Book of Jonah not only foreshadows Christ[17] but also anticipates the salvation of the nations.

---

16   This is likely the reasoning for Paul himself to venture to Spain (Rom. 15:24). Often it is proposed that, for Paul, this would (symbolically) be seen as the furthest known place, but that is unlikely. Given that Britian had been under Roman rule (more or less) for almost a century, land existing beyond Spain would be common knowledge. What is more convincing is that Paul saw himself as walking in the footsteps, thematically, of Jonah, fulfilling the call to all of the nations.

17   The "sign of Jonah" is the exclusive one provided to the nation (Matt. 12:39; 16:4; Luke 11:29–30). See David R. Scott, "The Book of Jonah: Foreshadowings of Jesus as the Christ," *BYU Studies Quarterly* 53.3 (2014), 161–180. See also Elizabeth Struthers Malbon, "Jonah, Jesus, Gentiles, and the Sea: Markan Narrative Intersections," in *Reading the Gospel of Mark in the Twenty-First Century*, ed. Geert Van Oyen (Leuven: Peters, 2019), 251–295; Joel E. Anderson, "Jonah in Mark and Matthew: Creation, Covenant,

That Peter finds himself in Joppa is no coincidence. During his stay, he receives a vision that will lead to the Gospel being opened to the Gentiles (chapter 10). Peter later recounts this experience to fellow Jewish believers (Acts 11:1–18), and in the second half of chapter 11, we see Hellenists—Jews who had adopted the Greek lifestyle and largely abandoned Jewish ways—coming to believe (Acts 11:20–21). In Acts 13, Paul and Barnabas are set apart by the Holy Spirit and sent on their mission (Acts 13:2). The narrative then further develops the theme of the Gospel reaching proselytes, Godfearers, and Gentiles. Paul and Barnabas proclaim that they are now turning to the Gentiles (Acts 13:46–47), marking a significant thematic shift that reverberates throughout the rest of Acts. This leads to the Council of Jerusalem in chapter 15, where the early Church debates the requirements for Gentile believers—particularly whether circumcision should be required for them. The book continues to trace the Gospel's spread throughout the Mediterranean through Paul and his companions.

What becomes increasingly clear is that Acts is built upon the theme of the Gospel's constant expansion: the faith once limited to elect Israel and those who joined her, is now extending to people of every nation. As Peter boldly states, "Truly I understand that God shows no partiality (*prosōpolēptēs*), but in every nation (*ethnei*), anyone who fears him and does what is right is acceptable to him" (Acts 10:35). The apostle's words are confirmed when the Holy Spirit falls on Cornelius and his household (Acts 10:44), much to the surprise of the Jewish believers: "And the believers from among the circumcised who had come with Peter were amazed, because the gift of the Holy Spirit was poured out even on the Gentiles" (Acts 10:45). This final remark is important to note and echoes the background information we have

Christ, and the Kingdom of God," *BTB* 42.4 (2012), 172–186.

touched on. A new era has begun. The Gentiles have received their own Pentecost, and their inclusion becomes the theme of all of Acts. The entire narrative must be read in light of this truth: Israel's borders are enlarged to receive the ingathering of the nations. Prophecy is being fulfilled in Christ, by the Spirit.

Reconsidering the Meaning of Peter's Vision

The first major turn in the Church's salvation-history—and one of immense importance for arguments about the Law's application for believers—is certainly Peter's vision in Acts 10. To restate the common interpretation: many believe that in this moment, God made both Gentiles *and* unclean animals clean, thereby granting believers permission to eat whatever we desire. However, two glaring issues emerge immediately. First, as we've already stressed, the narrative never states that unclean animals were made clean, nor did the early Church interpret the vision that way. This conclusion is drawn by way of inference, not by way of a simple reading of the text. Second, Peter's response within the story presents a serious challenge. As I mentioned in Chapter 1, did Peter somehow miss the memo when he refused to eat the animals shown to him (Acts 10:14)? Considering this event likely occurred a decade after Mark 7—where Jesus is said to have made all foods clean—wouldn't Peter have recalled such a pivotal declaration? The sharpness of Peter's objection to God is difficult to explain unless he genuinely believed he was upholding the Law's commandments concerning clean and unclean foods, which he still regarded as valid and binding. These two problems highlight significant flaws in the common interpretation. A closer reading shows that the vision has nothing to do with animals in the way it is commonly understood.

Jonah, Joppa, Gazelles, and Gentiles

Though the vision itself is found in Acts 10:9–16, the contextual environment begins in Acts 9. There, following Paul's conversion (Acts 9:1–35), the story picks up with Peter in Joppa, the coastal port city of Israel. In Joppa, a female disciple had died, and Peter, called by the other disciples, came and prayed "Tabita, arise." The lady, Tabitha (called Dorcus), was resurrected (Acts 9:40). There is likely wordplay here with *tabeitha anastēthi* and that of Jesus's *talitha cumi* in Mark 5:41, positioning Peter as continuing Jesus's ministry. There, Mark parenthetically adds that the phrase in Aramaic means "Little girl, I say to you, arise." In both the Aramaic *tabeitha* and the Greek *dorkas*, the lady's name means "gazelle," which may carry more wordplay: in the OT, the gazelle is used in Song of Songs in a positive light (2:9, 17; 4:5; 7:3; 8:14), and the Hebrew word, *tsebiy*, is defined as "beauty," "glory," "honor," etc., along with "gazelle." As we will see below, animals carry significance in both the Hebrew Bible and Second-Temple-Period literature. The word for "deer" (*'ayâl*) often overlaps with that for "gazelle," and we find the deer in symbolic places: both in Psalm 42:1, "As a deer pants for flowing streams, so pants my soul for You, O God," and in the eschatological chapter of Isaiah 35, where blind eyes will be opened and deaf ears hear (Isa. 35:5). Isaiah then continues:

> then shall the lame man leap like a dear, and the tongue of the mute sing for joy. For waters break forth in the wilderness, and streams in the desert; the burning sand shall become a pool, and the thirsty ground springs of water; in the haunt of jackals, where they lie down, the grass shall become reeds and rushes. And a highway shall be there, and it shall be called the Way of Holiness; the unclean shall not pass over it. It shall

belong to those who walk on the way; even if they are fools, they shall not go astray. No lion shall be there, nor shall any ravenous beast come upon it; they shall not be found there, but the redeemed shall walk there. And the ransomed of the Lord shall return and come to Zion with singing; everlasting joy shall be upon their heads; they shall obtain gladness and joy, and sorrow and sighing shall flee away.

Isaiah 35:6–10

What we see here is a plethora of wilderness and animal language, and even a reference to the concept of clean and unclean. We will discuss the significance of animals below, but for now we will expand our search for parallelism. An interesting use of *tsebiy* ("gazelle" or "beauty") is found in Isaiah 4:2, which says, "In that day the branch of the LORD shall be beautiful and glorious, and the fruit of the land shall be the pride and honor of the survivors of Israel." The short chapter is eschatological in nature, foreseeing a time when God "washes away the filth of the daughters of Zion" (Isa. 4:4).[18] Moreover, the term "branch" (*tsemach*) is used for Jesus (Jer. 23:5; 33:15; Zech. 3:8; 6:12). Following this, Isaiah 4:5 uses language similar to that of the Sinai theophany and exodus-wilderness travels,[19] while verse six adds: "There will be a booth for shade by day from the heat, and for a refuge and a shelter from the storm and rain." Though often overlooked, this section seems to weave in a textual allusion to Jonah. Joppa is the city to which Jonah flees after God calls him to proclaim the truth to Nineveh, and Jonah

---

18   The mention of washing is interesting prior to a vision about God cleansing/purifying.

19   Here the text reads "Then the Lord will create over the whole site of Mount Zion and over her assemblies a cloud by day, and a smoke and the shining of a flaming fire by night; for over all the glory there will be a canopy." Eschatological Sinai images are present, as well as vocabulary.

hopes to travel to Tarshish by boat (Jonah 1:3). This is the very place where Peter now finds himself—on the coastland of Israel, perhaps reminiscent of OT passages.[20] It is also no coincidence that Peter was called "son of Jonah" (Matt. 16:17), adding to the theme.

In the book of Jonah Jonah, once the prophet had witnessed to the city of Nineveh and they had repented, he was oddly grieved, retreating outside of the city gates. It is suggested that Jonah was grieved over the city having repented (Jonah 4:2), which may have inspired his earlier flight to Tarshish, some speculating that Jonah feared God was turning away from Israel unto the Gentiles.[21] Whatever his exact reasoning, he desired his life to be taken (Jonah 4:3), prompting God to ask whether his anger was well placed (John 4:4). Jonah made himself a booth (*sûkkâh*) to sit under its shadow (*tsêl*) as he awaited the city's fate (Jonah 4:5). God sent a plant for further shade (Jonah 4:6), but then sent a worm to attack it (Jonah 4:7), and then sent a "scorching east wind" that beat down upon Jonah (Jonah 4:8). Once again, Jonah pleaded for death, and God asked if his anger over the plant was justified. Jonah insisted that it was—he said he was "angry enough to die" (Jonah 4:9). God rebukes him, saying that "You pity the plant, for which you did not labor, nor did you make it grow, which came into being in a night and perished in a night. And should I not pity Nineveh, that great city,

---

20   Psalm 97:1; Isaiah 11:11; 24:15; 41:1, 5; 42:4; 49:1; 51:5; 66:19; Jer. 31:10. See also Isaiah 60:9 with the connection of Tarshish. Such a focus is beyond our limited scope, but adds to the imagery.

21   Jonah, though its date (and historicity at large) is challenged and unknown, was likely written in one of the many periods of Israelite disobedience and covenantal unfaithfulness. It is possible here that Jonah felt God, as many have commented on Jonah knowing he is good, was preparing to abandon Israel and turn to the nations. Thus, if he went to Nineveh and preached repentance, and they did indeed submit to God, that the Lord would turn to them, or enable them to punish Israel.

which there are more than 120,000 persons who do not know their right hand from their left, and also much cattle?" (Jonah 4:10–11). This event is mostly ambiguous, but holds some symbolism.

The textual similarities between Isaiah and Jonah are seen in the use of the words "booth" (*sûkkâh*) and "shade" (*tsêl*). Jonah constructed for himself a "booth" to shield himself from the heat of the day, and in Isaiah God will provide "a booth for shade by day from the heat" as well as "a refuge and a shelter from the storm and rain" (Isa. 4:6). While it would be inappropriate to press the parallelism here too far, it is noteworthy. Though "heat" is absent in Jonah, it is implied, and it is particularly evident from God sending the "scorching east wind," which made "the sun beat down on the head of Jonah so that he was faint" (Jonah 4:8). The whole imagery here reinforces the central theme of Jonah: the repentance and salvation of the nations. Just as striking is Jonah's—and likely Israel's—resistance to that divine act. As Douglas Stuart writes, "Jonah did not want Yahweh to do what was right and proper according to his merciful nature. Instead of showing to Assyria the kind of undeserving favor he had granted to Israel, he should punish the Assyrians without giving them any chance to repent. The book's audience is hardly exempt from such thinking."[22] The plant provides terrible irony here in that Jonah expressed deep care and concern over it, but none for a city of over 120,000 souls who, sinful but ignorant, needed saving. God's rebuke is essentially this: "how can you, an Israelite mercifully saved—my enemy due to your continuous sin—place such value on your plant that you did nothing to earn, yet

---

22 Douglas Stuart, *Hosea-Jonah*, WBC 31 (Grand Rapids, MI: Zondervan Academic, 1987), 502. As Leslie C. Allen puts it, Jonah couldn't bear seeing Nineveh "enjoying honey from the Jewish hive" and that "This nationalistic prophet is running odiously true to type" (*The Books of Joel, Obadiah, Jonah, and Micah*, NICOT [Grand Rapids, MI: Eerdmans, 1976], n.p.), keeping with Jewish nationalistic attitudes.

show no compassion for these souls of Nineveh?" Despite not deserving it, Jonah was delivered from the fish (the exclusive sign of Jesus, cf. Matt. 12:39–40, 16:4; Luke 11:29–30) and given the plant for shade (likely a metaphor for Israel's protection and deliverance by God), but he was unwilling to have compassion for his enemies. But God *is* willing.

As with other eschatological sections of Scripture, "booth(s)" symbolize God dwelling with his people and often point to the inclusion of Gentiles in the time of restoration.[23] In this particular event, we see two other possible textual allusions. The first is the significance of an east wind (Jonah 4:8),[24] along with its effects on Jonah. As Stuart writes, "This wind may have been that sort called elsewhere the scirocco, i.e., constant hot air so full of positive ions that it affects the levels of serotonin and other brain transmitters, causing exhaustion, depression, feelings of unreality, and, occasionally, bizarre behavior," and complete with the heat of the sun beating down, "caused Jonah to experience sunstroke / heat prostration, the common symptoms of which are physical weakness and mental anguish."[25]

Peter, the son of Jonah, would also experience a type of "sunstroke"—a symbolic parallel—as well as demonstrate a reluctance to associate with those of the nations, the very people to whom the God of Israel was now revealing himself. Indeed, the themes in Jonah—particularly the reluctant extension of God's mercy to the nations—form a meaningful, though implicit, backdrop to Peter's experience.

---

23 See for example Amos 9:11–12, which is used by James in Acts 15:16–17.

24 The east wind dries up the vine in Ezekiel 17, which may carry symbolic significance here.

25 Stuart, *Hosea–Jonah*, 505–506. W. Dennis Tucker Jr. sees Jonah as experiencing sunstroke (*Jonah: A Handbook on the Hebrew Text*, BHHB [Waco, TX: Baylor University Press, 2018], 99).

In this light, Peter is implicitly portrayed as a kind of new Jonah: the prophet who initially resisted preaching God's message to the nations. Textual (semantic) and thematic (theological-narrative) parallels link the accounts, especially set against other eschatological passages in the OT."

What remains largely implicit is the semantic matrix of animal language used through the OT and just under the surface in Acts 9. Three factors justify exploring this further: (1) the widespread use of wilderness imagery and references to Gentile inclusion in eschatological passages, as briefly noted above; (2) the use of animals in Peter's vision; and (3) the recurring use of animals in Jewish literature to represent both Israel and the nations. As we will explore further below, perhaps the most striking example of this symbolism is *the Animal Apocalypse* of 1 Enoch, though similar use of animal language is also used in the NT, including in the words of Jesus himself. In Matthew 15, when a Canaanite woman pleads for help, Jesus responds that he was sent only to the lost sheep of Israel (Matt. 15:24), adding, "It is not right to take the children's bread and throw it to the dogs" (Matt. 15:26). While Jesus did help her, the dichotomy between sheep and dogs suggests more than just figurative speech in ancient Israel. Dogs have a mixed place in both the OT and NT. Paul, for example, uses the term to describe evil Jews and evildoers (Phil. 3:2), and John uses the term alongside a host of unfavorable terms (Rev. 22:15). It is possible that "dog" had become a generic and widely used derogative term in general (Deut. 23:18; 1 Sam. 17:43; 2 Kgs 8:13; 2 Pet. 2:22), but perhaps there is more to it. (We will discuss this more below.)

The antinomian interpretation of the vision at Joppa stands as one of the clearest examples of interpreters employing eisegesis, as there is nothing in the text that directly suggests the cleansing of animals. The animals included in the vision likely draw upon a zoomorphological background rooted in Jewish tradition. Understanding this background is necessary: just as the animals are lowered on a sheet before Peter, so too is the vision itself presented to us, the readers, upon a tapestry of interwoven themes, motifs, and imagery from Israel's history and God's unfolding redemptive plan. That God would use established Jewish literary tradition—particularly the imagery of animals—is not difficult to imagine. After all, he is confronting Peter's unbiblical belief that one must not associate with Gentiles (Acts 10:28). If Gentiles are being symbolically represented as animals, their "cleansing" becomes a striking rebuke of Peter's nationalism and his Jonah-like resistance to God's inclusion of the nations in Christ.

Peter's proximity to the boundaries of what was considered clean and unclean within Jewish tradition is highlighted by his staying in Joppa "for many days with one Simon, a tanner" (Acts 9:43). This detail is no accident. A tanner (*bursei*) was a leather worker, and while there is no indication that this involved unclean animals, the occupation itself was often viewed with suspicion. As Horatio B. Hackett comments, "The more scrupulous Jews regarded such an occupation as unclean, and avoided those who pursued it. The conduct of Peter here shows that he did not carry his prejudices to that extent."[26] By choosing to stay with someone considered ritually questionable ("common") by stricter Jewish standards,[27] Peter was already stepping beyond certain

---

26   Horatio B. Hackett, *A Commentary on the Original Text of the Acts of the Apostles*, rev. ed. (Boston: Gould & Lincoln, 1858), 174. See m. Šab. 1:2; m. Meg 3:2; b. Pesah. 65a (per Shnabel).

27   Schnabel (*Acts*, 822) disagrees with both a safe assumption that we can conclude tanners were considered unclean and adds that "it seems doubtful that Luke's comment on Simon's profession is meant to convey that Peter disregarded social or ritual boundaries, having overcome traditional Jewish scruples against contact with what was ceremonially unclean—which thus minimizes the main point of the following episode of Peter's

traditional boundaries and misplaced prejudices. This setting, then, becomes the perfect opportunity for God to correct one of *Peter's* misplaced prejudices—his resistance to associating with Gentiles.[28]

The second stage in the context of the vision is also no coincidence. While Peter is settling into the home of Simon the tanner, another key event is unfolding: the God-fearing Gentile Cornelius, a Roman centurion and someone who would have been considered ritually "common" by more scrupulous Jews, receives a vision from an angel. His prayers and alms are acknowledged as pleasing to God (Acts 10:4), and he is told to send men to Joppa to fetch "one Simon who is called Peter... lodging with one Simon, a tanner" (Acts 10:5–6). For our purposes, it is important to notice how all these seemingly minor details are beginning to build upon one another. Together, they form a mosaic of serendipitous situations surrounding Peter, while simultaneously preparing both the characters and us—the readers—for the developing play on God's salvation stage.

The Vision at Joppa

The mention of Cornelius likely echoes Jonah's "innocent" Ninevites. Should God not show mercy to this "devout man who feared God with all his household, gave alms generously to the people,

---

encounter with Cornelius, a pagan officer in the Roman army," and I would add the encounter altogether. Luke's intention is likely thematic. Peterson (*Acts*, PNTC, n/a) adds "Peter was apparently not troubled by such concerns [of Jewish tradition], but he would soon have difficulty taking the more radical step of visiting a Gentile household."

28   Isaac W. Oliver ("Simon Peter Meets Simon the Tanner: The Ritual Insignificance of Tanning in Ancient Judaism," *NTS* 59.1 [2012], 50–60) has persuasively argued against tanning transmitting ritual impurity. If reflective of conventional, yet unbiblical, views, this would seem to be a hint towards this larger theme of God overturning Peter's prejudices which stem from Jewish tradition. That the two share the same name (Simon) likely carries significance as well.

and prayed continually to God" (Acts 10:2)? The fact that Cornelius receives a vision at the same time not only affirms the validity of the entire situation but also sheds light on the nature of Peter's vision—Peter's vision, we might say, is a divine response to Cornelius's. Put another way, both visions are working toward the same goal: the full inclusion of Gentiles into the people of God. If that is the shared goal, then we can interpret all the narrative elements up to this point—including the details and nuances of Peter's vision—as preparation for the instructions Cornelius had already received. The two visions interpret and complete one another. Just as broader theological themes—such as those seen in Jonah and the symbolism of animals—help establish the background of the vision, so too does Cornelius provide the immediate theological context. This detail cannot go unappreciated.

Several ideas intersect here. The first is the structural nature and flow of Luke's writing and how he moves the narrative along through certain "theological intervals" that serve to carry the main theme forward. That Peter's Vision follows Paul's conversion is no accident and, as Dunn puts it, chapter nine "had interrupted [the flow of the gospel's expansion] to ensure that the conversion of Saul was given due and early prominence."[29] Like Dunn, Fitzmeyer sees this as "the connecting link between the story about Saul, the 'chosen instrument' for the Gentile mission, and the actual start of that mission, which Peter inaugurates."[30] In this view, the vision—at least thematically—serves to bolster and establish Paul and his gospel-to-the-Gentiles as legitimate, which is certainly true, at least in part. Donald Hagner points

---

29   James D. G. Dunn, *The Acts of the Apostles* (Grand Rapids, MI: Eerdmans, 1996), 170.

30   Joseph A. Fitzmeyer, *The Acts of the Apostles: A New Translation with Introduction and Commentary*, AYB 31 (New York: Doubleday, 1998), 443.

out the necessity for Peter to have been commissioned at first with the gospel to the Gentiles: "Had Paul, not one of the twelve, been the founder of the mission to the Gentiles, its propriety would forever have been suspect."[31] Focusing on Paul alone is clearly unfit, given Peter has his own story arc and development. As Stephen S. Liggins observes regarding Peter's speech in Acts 10:34–48, upon understanding the vision, it "could be viewed as a conclusion, summary or final word on his evangelistic ministry," going to the Gentiles, and with the event being "paradigmatic in the narrative for ministry to such audiences."[32]

Thus, Peter's vision must be understood as part of the larger material coalescing around a major theme of Acts, which is, as we have discussed, Gentile inclusion. As we have also discussed, a few observations must be made regarding the vision's content and context itself. First, we have noted that the interpretation of a dual-meaning—i.e., both Gentiles and animals are made clean by God—is strikingly missing from the account. In honest approach to the text demands that an alternative interpretation be seriously considered. Second, the person of Cornelius must be approached with nuance concerning with his beliefs. As Eyal Regev notes, "Cornelius is not a conventional Gentile but a pious God-fearer." He adds that, even unto Acts 15, "In my view, all or almost all these Gentiles were God-fearers and not suspected of idolatry" and even points out the detail that "throughout the narrative of Acts, there is no clear case in which a true pagan joins Christianity, and in most of the cases Luke makes it clear that the Gentile Christians were God-fearers."[33] The nature and extent of legal observance of

31 Donald Hagner, *How New is the New Testament? First-Century Judaism and the Emergence of Christianity* (Grand Rapids, MI: Baker Academic, 2018), 59.

32 Stephen S. Liggins, *Many Convincing Proofs: Persuasive Phenomena Associated with Gospel Proclamation in Acts*, BZW 221 (Boston: De Gruyter, 2016), 157–158.

33 Eyal Regev, "Jewish Legal Practice and Piety in the Acts of the Apostles: Apologetics

Godfearers is often debated in scholarship,[34] but it plays an important role in situating the implications here. At the least, despite views to the contrary, it is unlikely that Cornelius, who is called "devout" (Acts 10:2) and "well spoken of by the whole Jewish nation" (Acts 10:22), would have disregarded the basic food laws. It is even more unlikely to imagine him preparing an unkosher meal for Peter, the Jewish apostle par excellence, in his own home. Though eating is never mentioned in the account,[35] the typical assumption that Peter's vision results in him entering Cornelius's house and eating unkosher food needs serious reconsideration.

Another significant aspect of the narrative is Cornelius being a Roman, and not only that, but a centurion. The inclusion of this Roman centurion—the quintessential enemy of first century Jews— would be the pinnacle, the apex, of the centrifugal and inclusive Jewish gospel to the Gentile world.[36] This detail further locates the vision in its proper salvation-historical and ecclesiological context in which it should be read. Not to be missed, too, is the falling of the Spirit upon these Gentiles (Acts 10:44–46), mirroring the Jews' own Pentecost experience some chapters ago. This detail, again, grounds the intended meaning of the vision in the inclusion of Gentiles into the people of

---

or Identity Marker?" in *Religious Stories in Transformation: Conflict, Revision, and Reception*, ed. Alberdina Houtman, Tamar Kadari, Marcel Poorthuis, and Vered Tohar, JCP 31 (Leiden: Brill, 2016), 131,133.

34 See the dated, but sufficient extended discussion in Irina Levinskaya, *The Book of Acts in Its Diaspora Setting*, BAFCS 5 (Grand Rapids, MI: Eerdmans, 1996), 51–126. See also the succinct work in Ross S. Kramer, "Giving up the Godfearers," *JAJ* 5.1 (2014), 61–87.

35 F. F. Bruce, *The Book of Acts*, NICNT. rev. ed. (Grand Rapids, MI: Eerdmans, 1988), 220.

36 Alexander Kyrychenko, *The Roman Army and the Expansion of the Gospel: The Role of the Centurion in Luke-Acts*, BZW 203 (Boston: De Gruyter, 2014); Laurie Brink, *Soldiers in Luke-Acts: Engaging, Contradicting, and Transcending the Stereotypes*, WUNT 362 (Tübingen: Mohr Siebeck, 2014).

God, putting the focus on the role of the Spirit in sanctification and salvation for all peoples.[37]

A third point, which is often entirely overlooked, is that Peter's vision concerning animals and food/eating occurs precisely when Peter "became hungry and wanted something to eat," while "they" were in the process of preparing a meal (Acts 10:10). As F. F. Bruce observes, there is no doubt that Peter's hunger was about food due to Peter's hunger.[38] Although some, like Pervo, suggest Peter may have been fasting,[39] this is unlikely.[40] John R. L. Moxon, who provides perhaps the most thorough treatment on Peter's vision and its relevant historical and contextual background, also highlights this detail: "That Peter is hungry and dreams of eating is a very simple consequence of natural dream theory, but is either ignored or viewed as contrived irony." He argues it should not be dismissed, noting that "this is a prominent co-location of detail."[41] The fact that Peter's vision corresponds so closely to his physical state—being hungry and experiencing a vision centered on food—further reinforces that the purpose of the vision is not intended to abrogate food laws. Rather, it suggests that the vision is personal and situational, directed to Peter in preparation for God's immediate purposes.

---

37 See especially the work by Amos Yong, *Mission After Pentecost: The Witness of the Spirit from Genesis to Revelation* (Grand Rapids, MI: Baker Academic, 2019), 171–80. Also, Gregg R. Allison and Andreas J. Kötsenberger, *The Holy Spirit* (Nashville, TN: B&H Publishing, 2020).

38 Bruce, *Acts*, 205. We will discuss this throughout our present treatment.

39 Pervo, *Acts*, 269.

40 Craig S. Keener, *Acts: An Exegetical Commentary*, 4 Vols. (Grand Rapids, MI: Baker Academic, 2013), 2.1762. All following quotations from Keener's work are from Vol. 2.

41 John R. L. Moxon, *Peter's Halakhic Nightmare: The "Animal" Vision of Acts 10:9 – 16 in Jewish and Graeco-Roman Perspective*, WUNT 432 (Tübingen: Mohr Siebeck, 2017), 178.

A fourth and generally important point is the complete absence of any OT mention or prophecy regarding the abrogation of the food laws. While, as discussed earlier, apostolic authority could theoretically permit a change to such a commands within the Law, one would reasonably expect some form of general theological justification for doing so, especially in light of passages like Amos 3:7: "For the Lord God does nothing without revealing His plan to His servants the prophets." Even if this is interpreted strictly in a prophetic sense, other changes in the Law throughout Scripture are typically accompanied by clear spiritual, theological, or ecclesiological rationale.[42] Some point to the rabbinic text *Midrash Psalms* 146:7 as evidence for changes in the dietary commandments. However, (a) rabbinic ideas about modifications to the Law are a later tradition altogether, and (b) the changes referenced in that context are clearly eschatological—linked to "the new creations"—and therefore disqualify any attempt to apply them in a present-day setting.[43] Taking an organic, whole-Bible approach, it becomes difficult to establish solid grounds for the abrogation of the dietary commandments. One basic but important question to ask

---

42 And these "changes" are minimal. To our knowledge, only the cultic commandments have undergone significant and reasonable "change," which the Epistle to the Hebrews argues for in consistency with the OT. Any other "commands" that have been "annulled" are only done so on a strictly circumstantial basis. For example, the commandments surrounding judicial and civil decisions cannot be applied in a setting where another government is in place. Paul, however, quotes the stoning verse of Deut. 17:7 in 1 Cor. 5:13 for casting out the sinner. This is an example of the Law still applying, even if its interpretation must be nuanced. One will be hard pressed to find any commandments that have been specifically abrogated, as in eternally, except that which is cultic.

43 See Keener, *Acts*, 1773: "[t]his tradition is probably too late to constitute background for this text." Also, "The entire theme of adaption in the Torah in the eschatological era… is mainly late and rare" (1773n441). It should be noted that this is the only found tradition of the food laws changing.

is: have the animals themselves changed? As previously discussed, one reasonable interpretation of the dietary and hygienic laws is that they are rooted in health, biology, and the natural order. In the eschatological age, nature itself is presumably changed—but that age has not yet arrived.

Another key detail we have already touched on is Peter's vehement—and nearly audacious—refusal to obey God's command to eat, as well as his complete bewilderment regarding the meaning of the vision. This second point is perhaps even more revealing for our interpretation. As mentioned earlier: did Peter somehow miss the message of Mark 7? And if Peter—who had lived closely with Jesus for years—was bewildered by the vision's meaning, how can modern readers be so certain of its interpretation, especially when the text itself gives no indication that the animals were being cleansed? The problem, first and foremost, lies in poor reading. The vision is clearly "an allegorical vision—a vision that does not make sense in itself, but requires interpretation," and, accordingly, "The reader is not encouraged to take this vision at face value—a divine statement overturning food laws—because Peter does not even consider this as an option."[44] As Craig S. Keener observes, "the unfolding narrative interprets the imagery in a manner distinct from the way one might construe it taken by itself."[45] But even this assumes that the idea of abolishing the dietary laws was something conceivable—which, for the Second-Temple-Period Jew, it was not. Such an enormous change would demand unmistakable clarity. Yet modern interpreters often rest their conclusions on assump-

---

44 John B. F. Miller, *Convinced that God Had Called Us: Dreams, Visions, and the Perception of God's Will in Luke-Acts*, BibInt 85 (Leiden: Brill, 2007), 207, 208. See Miller's large work for the need to appreciate the interpretive value on the receiving person's end. We will discuss this point below.

45 Keener, *Acts*, 1773n443.

tion—essentially constructing a "double vision" interpretation that is neither clearly stated nor even implied. That this remains a dominant view is, in itself, difficult to explain, as it is so poorly supported that one might wonder how it ever gained traction at all.

Yet, astonishingly, many still do. The majority of modern commentators interpret Peter's vision as signaling that the OT food laws have been done away with.[46] Unfortunately—and quite surprisingly— very few works dedicate significant time or analysis to the vision itself or to explaining how such an interpretive connection is actually made.[47] It is simply assumed. However, as we will demonstrate below, the text itself offers no justification for such a conclusion.

Returning to the text, the day after Cornelius received his vision and sent three men to fetch Peter, and just as those men were nearing their destination (Acts 10:9; 11:11), we read that Peter "went up on the housetop about the sixth hour to pray. And he became hungry and wanted something to eat, but while they were preparing it, he fell into a trance" (Acts 10:9–10). The word used here for "trance," *ekstasis*, is the same term used for Paul's vision in Acts 22:17. The full phrase, *epepesen ep' auton ekstasis*, translates to "fell into a trance" or "an ecstasy came upon him." Moxon devotes considerable attention to the nature of dreams, nightmares, and visions—particularly what he calls "anxiety dreams"—and their relevance to Peter's experience here,[48] which we

---

46   A handful of examples are Bruce (1998), Witherington (1998), Fitzmeyer (1998), Bock (2007), Peterson (2009), Schnabel (2012), Holladay (2016), etc. In fairness, Bock and Witherington admit, to some degree, that the vision may be a parable, yet both seem to implicitly maintain the typical view. To my knowledge, Jervell (1997, see esp. 306) is the only modern commentator who admits that the vision is not about food, and he maintains that they remained intact up to Acts 15, perhaps beyond.

47   Rather unsurprisingly, Keener's work is the most extensive and detailed treatment.

48   Moxon, *Peter's Halakhic Nightmare*, esp. 98–214.

will explore further below. In this state of ecstasy, Peter receives a vision in which "the heavens opened and something like a great sheet descending, being let down by its four corners upon the earth. In it were all kinds of animals and reptiles and birds of the air. And there came a voice to him: 'Rise, Peter; kill and eat.' But Peter said, 'By no means, Lord; for I have never eaten anything that is common or unclean.' And the voice came to him again a second time, 'What God has made clean, do not call common.' This happened three times, and the thing was taken up at once to heaven" (Acts 10:11–16). One of the first noticeable details of the vision is the appearance of a "great sheet" descending from heaven, accompanied by a voice. Whatever this object was, it prompts this question: would unclean animals—objects that defiled the Temple—be conceptually acceptable in heaven? Could we imagine such creatures residing there? While the text makes no mention of angels or the mechanism by which the sheet descends— and perhaps that's not the point—it is clearly being brought down to Peter's feet, directly from the heavens.

The mention of "animals and reptiles and birds of the air" (Acts 10:12) seems to echo the order of the Genesis creation account.[49] The phrase "all kinds" (*panta*) suggests the entire animal kingdom. The heavenly voice then commands Peter, "Rise...kill and eat." The three Greek terms used are *anastas* (rise), *thuson* (kill/slaughter), and *phage* (eat). Some commentators find significance in the wording of this command. For instance, Barrett suggests that *thuson* has a cultic connotation, implying sacrificial language with reference to the Temple.[50] While this is an intriguing possibility, the term lacks the lexical consistency to definitively establish such a connection. It is true that temple

---

49 Most commentators acknowledge the parallelism here.
50 C. K. Barrett, *Acts 1–14*, ICC (Edinburgh: T&T Clark, 2004), 507.

language is widely used in the NT to describe the church (e.g., 1 Cor. 3:16; 6:19; 2 Cor. 6:16; Eph. 2:11–21; Rev. 3:12), and Peter himself employs this imagery in 1 Peter 2:5. One might even argue that the Gentiles are being portrayed as offerings to God, in keeping with Paul's sacrificial language in Romans 15:16. However, this line of interpretation remains speculative. There is likely not too much to be gathered here from a lexical examination of the words. The command is straightforward: Peter is told to "arise"—possibly a motif of approaching God, a common use of this language, or simply a literal instruction to stand—and to "slaughter and eat." Peter's refusal is explicit: "By no means, Lord (*mēdamōs kurie*), because (*oti*) I have never eaten anything (*oudepote ephagon pan*) common or unclean (*koinon ē akatharton*)." This response closely matches the prophet Ezekiel's objection in Ezekiel 4:14, where, after being instructed to bake bread over human excrement, he refuses: "Ah, Lord God! Behold, I have never defiled myself. From my youth up till now I have never eaten what died of itself or was torn by beasts, nor has tainted meat come into my mouth." In fact, the phrase *mēdamōs kurie* ("by no means, Lord") is identical to that in the LXX version of Ezekiel, suggesting that Peter may be consciously aligning himself with the prophetic tradition of Ezekiel.[51]

The reason behind Peter's refusal seems plain. As Keener notes, the vision "would present a horrifying situation for any first-century Palestinian Jew."[52] The collection of animals includes both those described as clean and unclean, as confirmed by Peter's response: he declares that he has never eaten anything "common" (*koinon*) or "unclean"

---

51 Most commentators take note of this. The exclusion of "God" for Peter versus Ezekiel, if Peter has this account in mind, may suggest that Jesus is the One behind the Voice in the Vision.

52 Craig S. Keener, *The IVP Bible Background Commentary: New Testament*, 2nd ed. (Downers Grove, IL: IVP Academic, 2014), 350.

(*akatharton*), indicating two distinct categories of impurity that we will examine further below. As we will also discuss, Jewish thought held that clean animals could become defiled through close association with unclean ones, which likely explains Peter's refusal even to eat animals that might otherwise be permitted. Notably, the text provides no description eating, reinforcing that the focus is not on food itself, but on what the vision symbolically represents.

Overall, the vision is deeply alarming to Peter and quite ambiguity. Beyond the issues surrounding the food laws, the presence of animals in the vision carries its own significance. Animals and beasts were often used across various cultures to symbolize irrational people.[53] However, here the symbol appears to point in a different direction, which we will explore in greater detail below. For now, attention must be given to the Voice's response to Peter's objection: "What God has made clean, do not call common" (Acts 10:15). The focus here is best understood in terms of Peter's perception. A more precise rendering of the statement would be, "not go on calling common." The message already seems simple: God is telling Peter to stop labeling these animals—whether all of them or some of them—as "common." God's concern is centered on this one criterion: common. The word used for "cleansed" or "made clean," *ekatharisen*, could potentially apply to both "common" and "unclean" categories, as there is no alternative Greek term which uniquely applies to each category, to our knowledge. As such, determining what exactly has been "made clean" or "cleansed" requires close attention to linguistic analysis and the context.

Luke notes that the vision occurred three times, and afterward, the sheet was taken back up into heaven. The repetition of "three" is a clear pattern worth noting. As soon as the vision ends, we read:

---

53   Keener, *Acts*, 1766n380

"Now while Peter was inwardly perplexed as to what the vision that he had seen might mean, behold, the men who were sent by Cornelius, having made inquiry for Simon's house, stood at the gate and called out to ask whether Simon who was called Peter was lodging there. And while Peter was pondering the vision, the Spirit said to him, 'Behold, three men are looking for you. Rise and go down and accompany them without hesitation, for I have sent them'" (Acts 10:17–20). Peter goes down, welcomes the men, and invites them in to stay. At this point, we're met with a striking and serendipitous change in tone. We move suddenly from the imagery of animals and eating to a very real and immediate scenario: while Peter is inwardly perplexed (*dieporei*) about the vision's meaning and actively pondering (*dienthumoumenou*) it, three men appear. Talk about serendipity.

So far we have an evident pattern of three, a detail which has only (to my knowledge) gone noticed by Keener who, too, sees an allusion here to Jonah and provides a table of parallelisms there.[54] The table below will show the patterns of three throughout the Vision:

Vision	Command	Vision	Command	Vision
Three	**Rise**	Animals	**Rise**	Three
times	**Kill**	Reptiles	**Go down**	men
	Eat	Birds	**Accompany**	

Two additional instances of "threes" ought to be mentioned. If we take Christ as the speaker in the vision, then we observe a trinitarian

---

54   Keener, *Acts*, 1730. For another article detailing the connection between Jonah and Peter in the Joppa account, see Robert W. Wall, "Peter, 'Son' of Jonah: The Conversion of Cornelius in the Context of Canon," *JSNT* 29.9 (1987), 79–90. See also Miller's refutation, though, on Wall's proposals for "parallel and sequential catchwords" between them (*Convinced that God Had Called Us*, 204n134).

dynamic: Christ gives the command, God performs the act of cleansing (Acts 10:15), and the Spirit speaks to Peter, instructing him to go with the men (Acts 10:19). Additionally, the broader narrative divides naturally into three sections: the vision of Cornelius (Acts 10:1–8), the vision of Peter (Acts 10:9–16), and the revelation and speech of Peter (Acts 10:34–48). One could also see the third part as the actual meeting between Peter and Cornelius's household, or even the explanation of the vision to the Jewish believers in Acts 11:1–18. Regardless of how it is divided, the entire episode has a clear threefold structure.[55] Most striking, however, is the repetition of the three-part command structure. In the vision, Peter is told to "rise, kill, and eat" the animals. Shortly after, he receives another command: "rise, go down, and accompany" the men. Placing these two sets of commands side by side reveals a deliberate structural parallel:

Command in the Vision	Command in Interpretation
Rise (*anastas*)	Rise (*anastas*)
Kill (*thuson*)	Go down (*katabethi*)
Eat (*phage*)	Accompany (*poreuou*)

Interestingly, the only difference between the two threefold commands in the vision lies in the middle term of each: "kill" and "go down." While "eat" and "accompany" are not identical, there is a touch of irony and possible wordplay here, especially considering that the episode ends with Peter accompanying Cornelius and his household. Still, as previously discussed, the text never mentions actual eating—nor should the idea of consuming unclean food be assumed as the meaning. Rather, "eating" could function as a metonymy for table fellowship.

---

55 The significance of three for the sake of trinitarian implications here cannot be overstated.

The structure of the commands may be intentionally parallel: the first command, "rise, kill, and eat," mirrors the second, "rise, go down, and accompany." "Kill" and "go down" reflect immediate actions Peter is to take following the initial "rise," while "eat" and "accompany" point to the broader outcome of the event. In other words, both commands are essentially communicating the same message, though the first understood within its symbolic expessionism. What is most important to observe at this point is that the repeated threefold pattern serves as a deliberate literary device. It connects the meaning of the vision to the timely arrival of the three Gentile men—right as Peter is still trying to understand the vision—complete with another threefold command.

Some have suggested that the threefold repetition of the vision is tied to Peter's past—specifically, his threefold denial of Jesus (Matt. 26:69–75; cf. 26:35), followed by Jesus asking him three times if he loved him and instructing him to feed his sheep (John 21:15–17). While this connection may be valid, it is often presented with a negative undertone. That is, the repeated vision is seen as a response to Peter's stubbornness or resistance—perhaps even his failure to grasp what Jesus declared in Mark 7. One example of this interpretation is offered by R. L. Solberg,[56] who argues that the threefold repetition of the vision reflects Peter's hard-headedness and history of resistance. While not impossible, this line of reasoning remains speculative and places a heavy interpretive burden on the narrative. From a literary perspective, it seems more plausible that the threefold nature of the vision is meant to establish its interpretive connection to the arrival of the three men. Given Peter's bewilderment of and pondering on the vision's meaning, it is unlikely he would see the appearance of three

---

56 R. L. Solberg, *What God Has Made Clean: Why Christians Are Not Required to Keep Kosher* (Nashville, TN: Boyle & Co. Publishing, 2023), 51.

men at that exact moment as mere coincidence. Solberg, uniquely, contends that if the vision were only a metaphor for the inclusion of Gentiles and not *also* about food laws, then "the commands 'kill and eat' (v. 13) and 'What God has made clean, do not call common' (v. 15) would be based on a falsehood. God would be communicating to Peter that formerly unclean people are now clean by falsely declaring that previously unclean food is now clean. And God does not engage in false advertising."[57]

Solberg's position is, again, quite unique—I have yet to encounter anyone who shares his view. Given that Peter lived in a world steeped in enigmatic visions,[58] he would not find such an experience on the rooftop unfamiliar, even if the vision remains ambiguous to us. That Peter was left "perplexed" by the vision is entirely consistent with both the text and the cultural context. It does not imply that he was resisting a supposed message about animals or food; rather, it reflects the normal process of interpreting a divine encounter within his worldview. Solberg maintains that interpreting the vision as referring to people but not food reflects "an arbitrary standard based on a precommitment to keeping the kosher food laws,"[59] suggesting that such readers reject a dual interpretation out of bias. However, it is actually Solberg who imposes modern, Western expectations onto a first-century, Jewish context. This approach is itself arbitrary and reveals a deep disconnect from the cultural and religious environment in which Peter lived

---

57 R. L. Solberg, *Torahism: Are Christians Required to Keep the Law of Moses?* rev. ed. (Franklin, TN: Williamson College Press, 2019), 180–181, emphasis original.

58 Animal visions, even of eating them, are by no means novel. See for example the bad omen dreams of eating donkey meat in the ANE; Kenneth C. Way, *Donkeys in the Biblical World: Ceremony and Symbol*, HACL 2 (Winona Lake, IN: Eisenbrauns, 2011), 29–31, 101.

59 Solberg, *Torahism*, 180.

and from which his beliefs emerged. In short, Solberg's view is anachronistic. John B. F. Miller, in his focused study on dream-visions in Luke-Acts, remarks that these visionary experiences emphasize not just God's involvement in human affairs but also the necessity of human interpretation. He writes that while dream-visions depict "God's active involvement in the events of human history...it is equally important to notice the role of human interpretation in these encounters. Just as Luke's dream-visions depict God as an active participant in human affairs, they also depict God's people attempting to perceive God's will through these same visionary encounters."[60] Miller even shows that in the ancient world, there was often hesitation toward dreams and visions precisely because of the potential for misinterpretation. For Peter, that would mean depending on the Spirit's guidance—which, as we see in Acts 10:19, is exactly what happens.[61]

Miller adds, When one focuses too much on the divine side Luke's story [sic], one misses the fullness of Luke's message. Part of appreciating the fullness includes understanding the relationship between visionary experiences and the characters' perception of God's will throughout Luke-Acts."[62] This is not to say that the Spirit is downplayed or treated secondary in the role of revelation. Quite the contrary, the Spirit steps in to ensure one does not falsely interpret visions.[63] That we see no clarification of the narrative in Peter's Gentile-exclusive interpretation of the vision—no "hey, Peter, that vision was also about unclean animals"—confirms that it is to be interpreted the way Peter does. The silence is deafening to a dual-interpretation position. Miller

---

60   Miller, *Convinced*, 20.

61   Miller, *Convinced*, 63.

62   Miller, *Convinced*, 107.

63   Miller, *Convinced*, 111–124, esp. the notes.

actually demonstrates that taking a vision in Luke-Acts at face value is exactly the opposite of what Luke's narrative depicts, such as the story/vision of Mary in Luke 1–2, which "flies in the face of any suggestion that dream-visions nullify the role of human perception and interpretation."[64] The fact that no "correction" or "alternative revelatory interpretation" is to be found in Luke's account in or around Acts 10 betrays his writing and narrative style—if there was something "incomplete" or "incorrect" about Peter interpreting the Vision as being exclusively about Gentiles, Luke would have made mention of it.

In the case of Acts—and Peter specifically—Miller comments that "characters respond to their visions with some confusion and later offer dramatic interpretations of these experiences,"[65] a pattern that is represented perfectly in Peter's vision in Acts 10. Regarding the vision, Miller adds, "The allegorical nature of [it]...is not immediately apparent; it becomes clear only in Peter's interpretation of his experience found later in the narrative (Acts 10:34–35). Initially, Peter responds to the allegorical elements of the vision as literal commands,"[66] a blunder committed by modern interpreters as well. To be sure, "it is Peter's *interpretation* of his vision that is significant for the events that follow,"[67] and it seems Luke situates the narratological and theological weight upon Peter's coming to realize what the vision means. Peter's exclusive role as interpreter, however, *is* downplayed in the account by way of the voice and subsequent revelation provided to him, emphasizing "divine initiative" and the teachings promised to Cornelius by God.[68]

---

64   Miller, *Convinced*, 132.

65   Miller, *Convinced*, 167

66   Miller, *Convinced*, 207.

67   Miller, *Convinced*, 211; emphasis original.

68   Miller, *Convinced*, 214; cf. Acts 10:8.

Moxon, who provides an in-depth examination of dream-visions and interpretive processes in antiquity, notes, "That Peter is taken off to Cornelius' house while still trying to make sense of the vision is also unusual," being quite different from the typical reception of visions in the ancient world. He adds, "Indeed, Peter's developing understanding is articulated by a series of rather theological statements ('I truly understand that...etc.'), which seem based as much on what happens in the house as on the dream itself."[69] Relevant to Peter's vision, Moxon also discusses the history of symbolic dreams, which "typically involves images of natural objects, animals, and people but also sometimes nonsensical or mythological elements...Rarely making sense as they stand, interpretation can involve symbolic readings of dream objects and/or actions in a similar manner to an allegory or riddle."[70] This description fits Peter's experience quite well. Moreover, in the case of "anxiety dreams," they often offered figurative rather than literal meanings.[71] Particularly relevant to our analysis of the threefold nature in the parallel commands—"rise, kill, eat" and "rise, go down, accompany"—is Moxon's observation that wordplay was a common phenomenon in ancient dream-visions and their interpretations.[72]

Based on the analyses provided by both Moxon and Miller, there are neither (a) any substantial issues with interpreting Peter's vision as having a singular meaning, nor (b) any credible support for Solberg's claims that such a singular meaning amounts to "false advertisement based on a falsehood." Given the allegorical and figurative nature of visions in antiquity, their frequent symbolic interpretation, the consis-

---

69 Moxon, *Peter's Halakhic Nightmare*, 40.

70 Moxon, *Peter's Halakhic Nightmare*, 110.

71 Moxon, *Peter's Halakhic Nightmare*, 191.

72 Moxon, *Peter's Halakhic Nightmare*, 411–412.

tent use of symbolic visions throughout the Bible, the role of human *halakha*, and Peter's conclusion that the vision pertains to Gentiles *alone* and not to food, such an interpretation is not only reasonable but fully in line with the Bible. Everything we know from the ancient context suggests that the nature and function of Peter's vision fit perfectly within his cultural world. In fact, the vision aligns so closely with established patterns of dream and vision reception in antiquity that injecting a dual interpretation—one that also involves the cleansing of unclean animals—disregards the entire historical and cultural framework from which it emerged. In quoting Edith Humphreys, Miller summarizes Peter's active role in interpreting the vision, the narrative structure which supports it, and the gradual progression of his understanding as follows:

> While it is certainly the case that God is presented as the main actor in this episode, human decisions and interpretations of divine visions are evident throughout. Unlike the technique of the apocalypse, the visions are not given an authoritative interpretation by an *angelus interpres*; rather, they are understood through the mediation, speeches, and unfolding events enacted by the human players in the drama. Moreover, Luke seems happy to import interpretation into the visions as the action develops, demonstrating how human understanding enriches the significance of the visions. The Cornelius-Peter episode is obviously about coming to understand God's purposes for the Gentile community, but at every step of the way, human thinking and action are involved. Thus, the visions do not present a fait accompli but are artfully presented and combined to lead the hearers within the story, and the readers of the story, to certain conclusions. The way in which Luke

carefully intertwines narrative, argumentation, and vision-report may stand as a picture of his view of the relationship between the human and divine—here we see cooperation rather than coercion, disclosure rather than determination.[73]

Much like the nature, content, and subsequent interpretation of the vision itself, Peter's reaction of being "perplexed" is entirely consistent with responses to visions in antiquity and stands as an important detail that challenges the typical antinomian interpretation. The Greek word for "perplexed" is *diēporei*, which means to "be greatly perplexed, be at a loss"[74] "to be quite at a loss,"[75] or even "utterly at a loss."[76] In the New Testament, this term appears exclusively in Luke's writings: in Acts 2:12, describing the crowd being perplexed over the event of tongues; in Acts 5:24, where the guards are perplexed over Peter's escape from prison; in Luke 9:7, where Herod is perplexed by Jesus; and in Luke 24:4, when the disciples are perplexed at finding the tomb empty. Other suitable translations include "bewildered," "amazed," or "stupefied"—and such reactions to visionary experiences were not unusual in the ancient world. Pervo points out, for example, that in the Greek novel *The Aethiopica*, a character named Thyamis has a dream-vision that initially causes him to be "perplexed," coming to a different understanding of it than what he had initially imagined, if taken at face value.[77] Although Pervo does not mention it, the word used in that story (*diaporōn*) is the same word translated as "perplexed"

---

73   Miller, *Convinced*, 216. Cf. Humphreys, "Collisions of Modes," 82.
74   BDAG, 235.
75   LS, 193.
76   Moulton, 94.
77   Pervo, *Acts*, 274n108. Pervo calls it the 'Ethiopian Story,' and also references 2Macc. 15:12–16.

in Acts 10:17. Likewise, as Miller points out, *diaporeō* appears in an ancient inscription referencing a man named Xenainetos, who awakens "perplexed" after receiving puzzling instructions in a dream-vision.[78] Peter's vision is not only reminiscent of those found in the Greco-Roman and ANE worlds, but *even shares the same vocabulary.* There is nothing within Peter's vision itself—nor within its biblical or cultural environment—that suggests it cannot mean something *other* than what it first appears to be on the surface. In fact, this is precisely how the narrative itself unfolds: the symbolism gives way to the deeper meaning through Peter's eventual interpretation.

Whether Peter had discerned the meaning of the vision when Cornelius's men arrived, during the journey, or only upon entering Cornelius's home is uncertain. What Luke records is that upon arriving at Cornelius's house (Acts 10:25–27), Peter immediately makes a statement that, to the modern reader, might come across as a terribly impolite greeting: "You yourselves know how unlawful it is for a Jew to associate with or to visit anyone of another nation, but God has shown me that I should not call any person common or unclean" (Acts 10:28).[79] He follows this by explaining that, because of this revelation, he came "without objection" and then asks why he was sent for (Acts 10:29). Cornelius responds by recounting his own visionary experience (Acts 10:30–33). There is no doubt that this provided Peter with further confirmation—after all, unless Cornelius had spies tracking Peter, only God could have revealed his precise location in Joppa with Simon the tanner (Acts 10:32). After hearing Cornelius's account, Luke tells us, "So Peter opened his mouth and said: 'Truly I understand that God shows no partiality, but in every nation anyone who fears

---

78   Miller, *Convinced*, 208n144.

79   Imagine someone coming to *your* door and saying something like that!

Him and does what is right is acceptable to Him'" (Acts 10:34–35). Peter then relays Israel's salvation history, culminating in the person of Christ. Before he can even finish, he is (beautifully) interrupted as the Holy Spirit falls upon Cornelius and his family (Acts 10:36–46), prompting Peter and his companions to respond by baptizing them (Acts 10:47–48).

As we have stressed throughout, a plain reading of the text yields a straightforward and obvious interpretation: Peter explicitly states that God has shown him, through the vision, not to call any *person* common or unclean. The narrative unfolds smoothly, leading Peter to understand that the vision allegorically applies to Gentiles. Nowhere is there any hint whatsoever of a dual interpretation involving food laws. Peter's seemingly awkward greeting further reinforces the vision's purpose by directly linking the vision to the inclusion of Gentiles.

As most commentators acknowledge, Peter's reference to it being "unlawful" to associate with (*kollasthai*—literally "to keep company with") or visit (*proserchesthai*—literally "to come unto; approach; be near") someone of another nation does not originate from any command found in the Law. The word translated "unlawful," *athemiton*, should not be confused with a direct violation of the Law; rather, it conveys something considered "strongly frowned upon"[80] or "taboo."[81] Peter is not citing the Law but rather invoking Jewish tradition. Before exploring this, it is important to note how the vision experience ends. Peter moves naturally from the ambiguous imagery of the vision to what, for him, becomes its clear and intended meaning: those of other nations are not to be considered common or unclean. In verse 34, his

---

80   Ben Witherington III, *The Acts of the Apostles: A Socio-Rhetorical Commentary* (Grand Rapids, MI: Eerdmans, 1997), 353.

81   Bruce, *Acts*, 209, amongst others. Bruce (209n34) notes that this is the best translation.

declaration, "Truly I understand" (*ep alētheias katalambanomai*—literally "of a truth I perceive"), signals a moment of full realization. While in verse 28 Peter may have begun to grasp the implications—that he should no longer avoid or refuse association with Gentiles—by verse 34, his understanding is full: not only are these Gentiles no longer to be seen as common or unclean, but anyone who fears God is acceptable (*dektos*) to him. A major shift has occurred in Peter's thinking—the vision has moved from the issue of mere association with Gentiles to the affirmation that they are fully accepted by God.

Two stages of intimacy with God are present in this passage, and many interpreters note the shift in force regarding the Gentiles' acceptability and nearness to the God of Israel. Peter appears to move from the (possibly derogatory)[82] term *allophulō* ("foreigner") in verse 28 to *en panti ethnei* ("in every nation") in verse 35. The use of "in every nation" likely reflects a deeper theological realization: Peter now sees the eschatological promise of the inclusion of the nations coming to fulfillment. God is showing "no partiality," a truth confirmed through the acceptance of this particular Gentile—a Roman centurion, no less. What complicates the dual-interpretation view is the fact that God has not cleansed all things indiscriminately. As Keener comments, "Not all Gentiles are included in 'what God cleansed'—only those 'cleansed' (15:9) and 'set apart, made holy' (26:17–18) by faith."[83]

Here, there seems to be a clear qualification regarding what God has cleansed—namely, Peter recognizes the one who "fears him" as

---

82 This is to say that this may have been an ethnically charged slang term in Judaism. Again, Bruce (209n34) comments that the word for "foreigner" here, *allophulos*, is used in the LXX for an uncircumcised Philistine, as well as used by Josephus (*BJ* 5.194) in paraphrasing the contents written on the sereg (the wall separating Gentiles from entering the Temple courtyard) around the Jerusalem Temple.

83 Keener, *Acts*, 1773.

acceptable to him. This further demonstrates the idea that the vision pertains specifically to an act of God upon a person who comes to him in faith. What is not being portrayed is a blanket or universal "cleansing"—neither of all animals nor of all people. Rather, the cleansing is contingent upon faith and a response to God. Throughout Acts and the NT, whenever Gentiles are addressed, they are always those who are *already* coming to faith and joining with Israel. Peter's interpretation of the vision is that those Gentiles who come to God through Christ—symbolized, perhaps, by the sheet as representing their gathering into one flock or into Israel—have truly been "made clean" by God. Therefore, Peter cannot call them "common." To apply the concept of cleansing universally to all animals, or to all people without qualification, is not only a misreading of the vision but also a significant hyperextension of the cleansing act itself. Such an interpretation fails to take into account the soteriological significance for those coming to God through Christ.

Peter's reiteration of Jesus's command to preach to all people (Acts 10:42), along with his statement that the prophets bore witness to the remission of sins for anyone who believes (Acts 10:43), emphasizes the universal and inclusive scope of the gospel. What is unfolding before Peter—through what we will argue is an eschatological-apocalyptic vision—is the fulfillment of the OT expectation of Gentile inclusion. He now perceives the true, and only, interpretation of the Vision. It is possible that Peter's own words in Acts 2:39 are echoing in his mind: "For the promise is for you and for your children and for all who are far off, everyone whom the Lord our God calls to Himself." Here, "those who are far off" extends beyond the Jewish Diaspora to encompass all the nations—"in every nation," as he now declares. Drawing from the OT prophets, Peter has plenty of source material to support such a conclusion, and he arrives at that conclusion with ease. Why many interpreters fail to do the same remains quite a mystery indeed.

But why would a vision about clean and unclean animals be used to represent Gentiles? While not unanimously agreed upon, the prevailing view is that Jews often regarded Gentiles as inherently unclean, or at the very least "common" (as will be discussed below). Though not stated explicitly in the limited historical sources we possess, the logic and context strongly support this inference. Peter's own words in Acts 10:28 affirm this point directly. Scholars commonly interpret the terms "associating" and "visiting" in that verse—terms that denote any kind of general social interaction or being in the company of Gentiles—as reflective of a concern over defilement through unkosher and unholy foodstuffs, among other things. As such, the dominant interpretation of the Peter's vision is that it addresses the issue of table-fellowship between Jews and Gentiles. The purpose, then, is to prepare Peter to "come unto" and share a meal with those who were not Jewish or proselytes.

The problem here is multifaceted, and the most accurate answer is, more or less, "all of the above." Strangely, the idea that the vision is primarily about Gentiles in general—meaning that they are no longer to be regarded as common and are therefore acceptable—is often overlooked. Scholarly discussions tend to focus heavily on varying levels of ritual purity, concerns about table-fellowship, and often extend into the assumption that Peter ate unkosher food with Cornelius and his family. As we have already discussed, this scenario is highly unlikely, especially in light of Cornelius's piety—a piety recognized even by Jews. It is even more unlikely to think Cornelius would have knowingly prepared an unkosher meal for his very Jewish guest. Moreover, Peter's statement in verse 28, "you yourselves know" (*umeis epistasthe*), regarding the Jewish taboo against associating with foreigners, reveals that Cornelius and his family were familiar enough with Jewish customs to be aware of the dietary regulations, if not keeping them themselves.

Though table-fellowship is certainly part of the goal, it is not the central point. As L. Scott Kellum notes, "Peter's reply did not address table fellowship directly. He reported the Lord's activity in saving these Gentiles, making table fellowship a moot point."[84] Any concerns about purity, table fellowship, or related matters are secondary consequences of the larger point—namely, that the Gentiles themselves had been made clean. This is the problem that the vision answers. The assumption that Peter would have immediately proceeded to eat unkosher food, or even that such an idea was meant to be drawn from the vision, fundamentally misses the point and is a construct of our own imagination projected onto the text. Keener offers a succinct overview of how Gentiles were perceived in terms of ritual uncleanness within Jewish thought.[85] He references sources such as *Pirkei DeRabbi Eliezer* 29, which strongly suggests that Gentiles were considered to emit uncleanness by their very presence.[86]

Despite limited direct data, a strong case can be made for this idea by turning to John 18:28. There we read, "Then they [the Pharisees] led Jesus from the house of Caiaphas to the governor's headquarters. It was early morning. They themselves did not enter the governor's headquarters, so that they would not be defiled, but could eat the Passover." The word used for "defiled," *mianthōsin*, is another term related to ritual impurity,[87] and should be understood in that context,

---

84   L. Scott Kellum, *Acts*, EGGNT (Nashville, TN: B&H Academic, 2020), n.p.

85   Keener, *Acts*, 1788–1791.

86   Keener (*Acts*, 1789n613) argues that later perceptions of Gentile impurity were simply the refining of ideas that were already well established.

87   BDAG, 650. BDAG includes, under (2), morally impure. See the use in Heb. 12:15 and Jude 1:8. See also the similar *memiasmenois* in Josephus, *Jewish War* 2.149.

aligning with what we explore further below. Though only implied in this passage, the underlying concern of the Pharisees—that simply entering a Gentile dwelling could render them impure—reflects a broader belief in the natural impurity of Gentiles. This idea, that one could be defiled simply by being under the same roof as a Gentile, is echoed both in the vision Peter receives and in the extant Jewish literature available to us. This concern forms the entire theme of the vision, especially as Peter interprets it. All the ingredients necessary to establish the association between Gentiles and ritual impurity are present, and it is reasonable to make the connection.

As Schnabel explains, at the very least, "observant Jews suspected that the Gentiles were most likely unclean and thus a source of defilement," and in this vision, "the Spirit now directs Peter not to make a distinction that he would normally make between pure Jews and morally impure and profane Gentiles."[88] The text gives the reader no permission to extend the interpretation beyond what is explicitly provided, including implications of food or table-fellowship. When we look at the various stages of Peter's interpretive journey—especially the Spirit's command, which parallels the vision's threefold pattern, telling Peter to go with the Gentile messengers who arrive just as he is pondering the vision—we are directed to interpret the vision precisely as Peter does. These moments serve as "interpretive steps," guiding Peter (and the reader) forward toward the intended meaning, which by the end, becomes quite clear.

Readings that run contrary to the clear message of Acts 10 often stem from "later ecclesiastical traditions," which make it difficult "to sort out such matters, since we tend, despite all efforts, to read Acts

---

88 Schnabel, *Acts*, 884, 858.

from the side of Galatians and later church history."[89] As Chris Miller further observes, "While 'later ecclesiastical traditions' have certainly appealed to this as the abrogation of kosher laws, they should carry far less weight than textual evidence in our hermeneutic. It is also true that we often read Acts from the side of Galatians, but when we look to Mark or Paul to explain Luke, I believe we do fundamental disservice to Luke and to ourselves. Such attempts to find harmony in our theology at the expense of our exegesis should raise red flags, especially among those who claim a high view of Scripture."[90] A plain reading of the text reveals that Peter's Vision in Acts 10—together with its surrounding context—clearly communicates a singular theological and ecclesiological meaning: it addresses the purity of Gentiles and their acceptance by God, all within a salvation-historical framework, not an ethical one. The Vision is descriptive, not prescriptive. Yet just beneath the surface, we may elucidate the meaning further.

Koinos and Akathartos

Intrinsic to understanding the animals in the vision is Peter's response to the command to eat. As we previously mentioned, his refusal echoes that of the prophet Ezekiel in Ezekiel 4:14, a passage also steeped in symbolism and theological significance. In Acts 10:14, Peter replies, "By no means, Lord; for I have never eaten anything that is common or unclean." The final two terms—common (*koinon*) and unclean (*akatharton*)—are particularly important and warrant careful attention, as they represent two distinct categories. Up to this point,

---

89   E. M. Humphrey, "Collisions of Modes? Vision and Determining Argument in Acts 10:1–11:18," *Semeia* 71 (1995), 81; see Miller, note below, for source of this quote.

90   Chris A. Miller, "Did Peter's Vision in Acts 10 Pertain to Men or the Menu?" *BSAC* 159.635 (2002), 316; Humphrey's quote comes from Miller's work here.

we have not addressed this directly. Textually, the majority reading follows *koinon kai akatharton*, with the conjunction *kai* ("and") linking the two. However, an alternate reading exists: *koinon ē akatharton* ("common *or* unclean").

The distinction between these two readings is not without significance.[91] The majority reading uses *kai* ("and"), while I argue the preferable reading is *ē* ("or"). The key difference lies in whether the terms common and unclean are joined conjunctively or disjunctively. Despite the majority reading of *kai*, there are compelling reasons to favor *ē*. First, these two terms must be differentiated, as they are clearly distinct in Jewish literature. Second, and more decisively, this is the reading Peter himself affirms in his retelling of the vision in Acts 11:8—a retelling that is essentially verbatim.[92] Editions that opt for *kai* effectively force Peter to either contradict or adapt his earlier experience, rather than having him simply retell it as it occurred. Interestingly, even editions that use *kai* in Acts 10:14 often retain *ē* in Peter's retelling, creating an apparent contradiction. A third and particularly noteworthy point builds on what we have already observed: in verse 15, the voice responds not by referring to "unclean" (*akatharton*), but specifically to "common" (*koinou*): "What God has made clean (*ekatharisen*), do not call common (*koinou*)." This suggests that God is addressing Peter's concept of "common" rather than the concept of "unclean." The distinction God makes is not between clean and unclean animals, but between what is common and not common.[93]

---

91 See the discussion in Mikeal C. Parsons, "Nothing Defiled AND Unclean: The Conjunction's Function in Acts 10:14," *PRSt* 27.3 (2000), 263–274. The conjunction *kai* can take multiple meanings such as "and," "also," "even," and, in some cases, "or."

92 See the table in Schnabel, *Acts*, 836–838. Peter recalls the "or" reading as original.

93 Important, too, is a proper reading of God's charge. A better translation here for *su mē koinou* is "do not (continue) to consider common," considering the present, active

Taken together, these three points strongly support (a) the adoption of the "or" reading and (b) the interpretation of common and unclean as separate categories of "impurity"—an especially relevant distinction in the context of the ethically charged separation between Jews and Gentiles.

The two words—*akathartos* ("unclean") and *koinos* ("common")—are distinct in meaning. *Akathartos* corresponds directly to the Hebrew term *tame*, which refers to prohibited ("unclean") animals. *Koinos*, on the other hand, has a different meaning. Derivatives of *koinos* are used in the NT to describe things that are shared or held in common—such as shared possessions (Acts 2:44; 4:32), a "common" faith (Titus 1:4), or "common" salvation (Jude 1:3). These uses place *koinos* in the semantic realm of *what is shared by the common populace*. It is worth noting, too, that the NT itself is written in *Koinē* Greek—literally, "common" Greek. The two most important NT occurrences of *koinos* for our purposes are Mark 7:2 and Romans 14:14. Although we have briefly touched on Mark 7 already, it warrants closer examination here. In Mark 7:2, the Pharisees observe that some of Jesus's disciples ate with hands that were *koinais*, that is, "defiled," meaning unwashed. Mark's parenthetical comments in verses 3 and 4 clarify that this concern arises not from Scripture but from Pharisaic tradition.

---

imperative *koinou*. As Clinton Wahlen ("Peter's Vision and Conflicting Definitions of Purity," *NTS* 51.4 [2005], 505–518) translates it, 'You must stop reckoning as "potentially defiled" what God has declared "clean"' (515). It is also important to note the use of *koinou*, rather than *koinos*, in the NT. *Koinou* denotes the action of being defiled (Matt. 15:18, 20; Mark 7:15, 18, 23) or defilement (Acts 21:28; Rev. 21:27). Note the use in Heb. 9:13 where "[t]he blood of goats and bulls, and the sprinkling of defiled (*koinou*) persons with the ashes of a heifer, sanctify for the purification of the flesh" does not depict the cleansing of that which is inherently unclean, but defiled. The sacrificial system did not cleanse unclean things but defiled things, i.e., a state of ritual "impurity," per Wahlen's translation above.

Understanding Jesus's critique in Mark 7 as a rejection of humanly conceived traditions of ritual defilement—not of biblical categories of clean and unclean—is essential for properly interpreting Peter's vision. David G. Peterson's comments demonstrate the error that arises from disregarding this context:

> What was implicit in the teaching of Jesus is now made explicit. The clean and unclean provisions of the law were temporary, designed to keep Israel a holy and distinct people, until the time when Jews and Gentiles could receive the forgiveness of sins and sanctification on the same basis, through faith (Acts 20:32; 26:17–18; cf. 15:9, 'having cleansed their hearts by faith'). By the time he explains the vision to Cornelius and his household, Peter recognises that he should no longer allow the Levitical laws to keep him from associating with Gentiles (v.28).[94]

A proper reading of *koinos* reveals that Peterson's attempt to link the accounts in Mark 7 and Acts 10 is, at best, tenuous. The contexts and concerns in each passage are fundamentally different, and the supposed abrogation of dietary distinctions in Mark 7 appears to have had little, if any, impact on Peter—strongly suggesting that no such abrogation actually occurred. Rather, the concern in Mark 7 revolves entirely around Jewish traditions, a framework Peter himself remains deeply embedded in during the events of Acts 10. Jesus's statements in Mark 7 are explicit and targeted specifically at ritual purity regulations based on Pharisaic tradition. This likely reflects his

---

94   David G. Peterson, *The Acts of the Apostles*, PNTC (Grand Rapids, MI: Eerdmans, 2009), n.p. See our discussion on Mark 7.

general attitude toward those human traditions (cf. Luke 10:7). As Schnabel admits, Luke "has no parallel to Mark 7:19 and nowhere asserts that the work of Jesus included the abrogation of the dietary laws"[95] To quote Matthew Thiessen, "Mark's story explicitly situates Jesus's words about impurity (and Mark's own claim about 'purifying all foods') within the debate about the Pharisaic tradition of washing hands before meals. Any reading that ignores this specific context and takes [it] to refer to all foods (kosher and nonkosher) will likely result in a serious misinterpretation of the passage…Any reading of this story that depicts Jesus as rejecting God's commandment to Israel to avoid eating unclean animals results in a Jesus who is irrational at best, and deeply hypocritical at worst. Is Mark so bumbling a narrator that he fails to notice this result?"[96]

Witherington notes that the terms *koinos* and *akathartos* refer to different types of impurity: the former denotes something "defiled by association with something unclean," while the latter refers to "something inherently unclean." He adds, "It may be true that no known ruling specified that clean animals were automatically made unclean by mere contact with unclean ones, but it stands to reason that this was often assumed to be the case in early Judaism. It was, after all, assumed in early Judaism that a person incurred uncleanness by mere contact with an unclean person, and it suggests that the 'common' animals in this case did require to be cleansed."[97] Since Peter is already quite steeped in tradition, this distinction must be handled with some nuance. Clinton Wahlen offers a more thorough examination of these

---

95 Schnabel, *Acts*, 855. However, he believes that Peter's statement in Acts 10:28 implicitly supports such a conclusion.

96 Matthew Thiessen, *Jesus and the Forces of Death: The Gospels' Portrayal of Ritual Impurity within First-Century Judaism* (Grand Rapids, MI: Baker Academic, 2020), 193.

97 Witherington, *Acts*, 350n95. See also Keener, *Acts*, 1769n302, 1772.

terms, identifying three categories: clean, unclean, and common. Only the first two—clean and unclean—are grounded in the Torah, where they describe intrinsic and permanent states. The third, "common," conveys the idea of a contracted, temporary, or ritual impurity.[98] For Wahlen, the closest parallel to Acts 10 is in 1 Maccabees 1:47, 62, which "describes changes in the Jerusalem cultus decreed by Antiochus IV (Epiphanes)." He explains further:

> The first [verse] refers to the sacrifice of 'swine and common animals' (ὕεια καὶ κτήνη κοινὰ). Goldstein translates κοινὰ in v. 47 as 'ritually unfit', meaning 'those which had not passed the stringent requirements required [sic] for Jewish sacrifices, which were much stricter than those for pagans'. Here, however, κοινὰ apparently refers to something other than the blemished but otherwise clean animals that Goldstein has in mind. The term is more understandable in light of the other occurrence (about which Goldstein is silent): 'But many in Israel were strengthened and resolved in themselves not to eat common animals (κοινὰ)' (v. 62). The next verse makes explicit that the result of eating koina is defilement (v. 63). It cannot be taken to mean the eating of unclean animals because this has been clearly referred to already in v. 48. Rather, the unusual designation must refer to eating clean animals which are somehow objectionable as food, not just acceptable as a sacrifice.[99]

---

98 Wahlen, "Peter's Vision," 510–511.
99 Wahlen, "Peter's Vision," 511–512; emphasis original.

Wahlen demonstrates this position further through the example of the elderly priest Eleazar, who was pressured to eat clean food and *pretend* that it was pork. Eleazar viewed this as defiling and refused.[100] Wahlen offers a concise yet insightful summary of the impurity associated with Gentiles and food obtained from them—an issue directly tied to concerns over Gentile association. In his view, *koinos* naturally refers to impurity acquired through contact or association, encompassing both Gentiles themselves and food sourced from them: in short, "defiled by association." He argues that the meaning of Peter's vision—potentially operating as a *double entendre*—is that "just as the animals were to be regarded as clean despite being mixed with the unclean, so Cornelius should be considered 'clean' despite remaining uncircumcised. Peter now understands the impropriety of applying such categories to people, viz. 'potentially defiled' (κοινοί) to God-fearing Gentiles and ('intrinsic) uncleanness' (ἀκάθαρτοι) to pagans."[101]

Jason Staples adds to Wahlen's argument by pointing out that the terms *koinos* and *akathartos* "tend to refer to separate domains defined by the opposing categories of pure/impure (or clean/unclean) on the one hand and holy/common on the other" and comments that "impure food cannot be holy, but clean food can be either common (=unsacred) or holy." He adds, "Sacrificial food [i.e. that which is (firstly) inherently clean] is both clean and holy, but an ordinary, non-sacred meal for Jewish laypersons by definition falls into the clean/common catego-

---

100 Wahlen, ibid.

101 Wahlen, "Peter's Vision," 515. Wahlen's comment here on "circumcision" is due to the fact, as he discusses (516–518), Gentiles who had not "fully converted," i.e., undergone circumcision, would still be suspect regarding their inclination towards idolatry, which would defile. Here Wahlen argues that Peter must not regard God-fearers, those removed from polluting idolatry, as "common" like pagans who are actually "unclean." See his Figure 1. God makes no distinction over "potentially defiled."

ry."[102] Christina Eschner similarly comments, "The English 'common' best reflects the Greek κοινός in this context, since it includes both a positive connotation of 'something one shares' and a negative sense of something 'ordinary, vulgar.' In this way, the English 'common' expressed both nuances of the word's meaning in one adjective."[103] The word denotes simultaneously what is foreign to Israel, belonging to the outside world, as well as something particularly vulgar—that which is regarded as unfit for consumption or handling.

Essentially, in alignment with Pharisaic conceptions of purity, what Wahlen, Staples, and Eschner are explaining is that there were two categories of impurity recognized in first-century Israel. The first category concerns what is inherently clean or unclean, as outlined in texts like Leviticus 11 and Deuteronomy 14. The second involves the distinction between what is holy and what is common, the latter referring to something ritually impure or defiled through association with the "common"—such as Gentiles, Gentile food, female impurity, or other sources of contamination, which varied and overlapped across different groups and situations.[104] This concept is evident in the writings of the Maccabees and likely mirrors the Pharisaic view found in Mark 7, as previously discussed.

Staples, like Wahlen and Eschner, sees the implications of these distinctions as holding significance for the relationship between Jews,

---

102 Jason A. Staples, "'Rise, Kill, and Eat': Animals as Nations in Early Jewish Visionary Literature and Acts 10," *JSNT* 42.1 (2019), 3–17, 12.

103 Christina Eschner, "Purity and Impurity of Food and People in Acts 10:1–11:18: Is the Abolition of Jewish Food Laws at the Center of the Cornelian Narrative?" in *Purity in Ancient Judaism: Texts, Contexts, and Concepts*, ed. Lutz Doering, Jörg Frey, Laura von Bartenwerffer, eds, WUNT 528 (Tübingen, Mohr Siebeck, 2025), 367–368.

104 See Wahlen. See also Colin House, "Defilement by Association: Some Insights from the Usage of KOINÓ/KOINÓΩ in Acts 10 and 11," *AUSS* 21.2 (1985), 143–153.

God-fearers, and Gentiles. He astutely observes that "modern scholarly conflation of the two categories in this passage is especially ironic in this light, as interpreters have straightforwardly shared Peter's assumptions rather than heeding the heavenly voice."[105] He points out that the purification in Acts 10 addresses the Jewish concern over whether Gentile believers—those previously considered common—can now be seen as holy. According to Staples, "Gentiles are no longer to be regarded as common or potentially polluting—God has made them both clean and holy,"[106] thereby affirming their full inclusion in covenantal fellowship with the Jewish believers. From this, a kind of double-edged sword emerges. On one side, the distinction drawn in Mark 7 is not Jesus dismissing the food laws, but rather his rejection of Pharisaic notions of purity—practices and boundaries that extended well beyond what the Bible actually prescribed regarding diet and ritual cleanness. These same assumptions appear in Peter's vision, especially in light of God's explicit statement about what he has cleansed. Here, the issue is not clean versus unclean but holy versus common. The underlying question, then, is whether Gentiles, drawing from first-century purity categories, were viewed as defiled. On the other side of this "sword," if *koinos* and *akathartos* truly represent separate categories, then reading the vision as an abrogation or "cleansing" of intrinsically unclean animals becomes not just unlikely, but nearly impossible to justify within the text's historical context.

What we are left with is an aspect of the vision that thoroughly distances itself from any interpretation that God cleansed animals described as unfit for consumption in the Law. On the contrary, the vision employs deeply Jewish theological language, imagery, and

---

105 Staples, "Animals as Nations," 13.
106 Staples, "Animals as Nations," 14.

concepts to construct a webbing of allusions pointing to the ritual cleansing of Gentiles from a state of perceived defilement according to unbiblical *traditions*. In this context, Gentiles are symbolically depicted as unclean animals, placed alongside the (implied) clean animals that represent Israelites or Jews. The vision portrays the unclean animals— again, symbolizing Gentiles—as potentially "defiling" the clean animals through association, reflecting the *traditional* Jewish concern about proximity-based impurity. This background makes sense of Peter's unique choice of language, particularly his statement that it is "unlawful" (*athemiton*)—that is, culturally taboo—to "associate" (*kollasthai*) with or "approach" (*proserchomai*) someone of another nation.

The term "unlawful" (*athemiton*) serves to situate the entire pericope within the context of Jewish tradition. While it may remain somewhat ambiguous whether Gentiles were universally regarded as unclean—ritually, morally, or both—it is clear that Jews, at the very least, perceived them as defiling. Eschner provides a helpful summary of both the situation and the broader scholarly debate:

> Regarding the impurity of gentiles in Acts 10:28, research is torn between an interpretation as ritual or moral purity. In fact, several moral commands such as fearing God, justice, and prayer (10:2, 4, 30–31) as well as charity (10:2; cf. 10:4, 31; and also 9:36; 24:17) are mentioned in this context. Nevertheless, the impurity of the gentiles in Acts 10:28 is more of a ritual-corporal than of moral nature. The immediate context of this statement about impurity is the rejection of close contact with gentiles. Thus, impurity has the clear function of regulating social contact. This is typical of ritual impurity, since the crucial difference between ritual and moral impurity consists in the fact that the former is transferrable

by physical contact. Therefore, one should avoid any physical contact with things and people perceived as ritually impure, as the Lukan Peter himself declares in 10:28a. The following statement in Acts 21:28 is consistent with such a characterization of gentiles as ritually impure. Here, Paul [supposedly] brought Greeks into the temple and thereby made this holy place 'common,' meaning he desecrated it (ἔτι τε καὶ Ἕλληνας εἰσήγαγεν εἰς τὸ ἱερὸν καὶ κεκοίνωκε τὸν ἅγιον τόπον τοῦτον). In contrast, moral impurity is usually not contagious and does not require physical separation, which is why it is hardly a reason for denying any close contact.[107]

What develops for us here is that God, in cleansing these "common" Gentiles, directly annuls the Jewish perceptions of Gentiles within their own purity-religious system which hindered any association with those outside of Israel. As Eschner further writes, "Here, the gentiles are defined by the term κοινός as 'common people,' in contrast to the Jews as the holy people."[108] As such, with special focus on Peter's use of the term "foreigners" (*allophulō*), "The demand to stop calling anyone 'common or impure' means, therefore, that no one should automatically be considered impure *because of his descent from gentiles*."[109]

Recognizing Peter's statement as referring directly to people—that is, Gentiles—not only aligns more clearly with the semantic and traditional context of the vocabulary used, but also rightly centers the

---

107 Eschner, "Purity and Impurity of Food and People," 365–368.

108 Eschner, "Purity and Impurity of Food and People," 375.

109 Eschner, "Purity and Impurity of Food and People," 376. Eschner provides a thorough overview of the conception of Gentiles as defiling, particularly in Second-Temple-Period literature such as Jubilees 22:10–24 to separate from the nations, specifically to not eat with them. See 376–379.

language on its true subject: the Gentiles themselves. By confronting Peter's deep-rooted adherence to unbiblical Jewish traditions surrounding purity and defilement, God directly challenges and dismantles Peter's harmful perception that Gentiles were inherently defiled and therefore unfit to receiving the Gospel or being included among God's people. The message is clear: Gentiles are not defiled, and no Jew is defiled by associating with them—for God has cleansed them. This general conflation of dietary and purity language naturally carries over into the very imagery of the vision itself. The unclean animals symbolically represent Gentiles, and this visual metaphor becomes the central means through which the vision expresses its meaning.

Animals, Gentiles, and the Nations

In Galatians 2:15, Paul states (presumably addressing Peter), "We are Jews, naturally, and not out of the nations, sinners" (my translation). The preposition translated as "from among" (*ex*) denotes origin,[110] and the verse itself reflects a prevailing mindset: those who are "of the nations" were viewed as inherently sinful. This succinctly captures the sense of superiority and exclusivity often associated with Jewish identity—Israelites were seen as "inside," while Gentiles were decidedly "outside." This notion runs throughout Jewish literature, with a particular emphasis on the distinction of Israel as "clean" and the nations as "unclean." Matthew Thiessen picks up on this when he writes, "The impure animals, then, function as a coded vision about God's purification movement among those who were formerly impure: the gentiles."[111] But what leads Thiessen to interpret the animals in the vision as "coded" references to Gentiles? While such symbolic use is

---

110   See *NCNU*, 151–158; 379–387; 680–691.
111   Thiessen, *Jesus and the Forces of Death*, 194.

well-attested in Jewish literature, it is curiously overlooked in many commentaries on Acts.[112] This oversight is quite alarming, especially given that many scholars who focus on early Jewish texts fail to recognize the thematic consistency of animal imagery in Acts 10 with similar motifs elsewhere. As I will argue, missing this connection shatters one's ability to properly understand Peter's vision.

As briefly mentioned earlier, the clearest depiction of the nations as animals appears in the *Animal Apocalypse* found in 1 Enoch. In this vision, the patriarchs, Israelites, and surrounding nations are depicted as various animals. Given that Peter's Vision in Acts also features animals and occurs while he is hungry, this connection becomes particularly relevant in understanding its imagery. However, I would argue that the explanation goes beyond mere physical hunger. Rather than God appealing only to Peter's bodily state, it is more likely that he draws on a familiar source domain rooted in Peter's own Jewish cultural and literary background. While Peter's hunger does play a role, it seems secondary to the deeper, symbolic framework shaped by Jewish tradition. Jason Staples explores this very concept in his article focused on the animal imagery shared between the *Animal Apocalypse* and Acts 10. He summarizes the relationship as follows:

> The patriarchs are portrayed as white bulls, with Israel represented as sheep. Of special interest for our purposes, however, is that the various nations neighboring Israel are depicted as Levitically unclean animals... The Ishmaelites and Midianites are depicted as wild asses (surely deriving from Gen. 16.12), the Egyptians as wolves, Edom and Amelek (Esau's descen-

---

112 Examples: Bruce (1988); Witherington (1998); Fitzmeyer (1998); Bock (2007); Pervo (2008); Peterson (2009); Schnabel (2012); Keener (2015); Holladay (2016).

dants) as wild boars, Ammon as foxes, the Babylonians as lions, the Assyrians as tigers/leopards, the Arameans as hyenas, and the several types of Greeks as various birds of prey.[113]

Staples sees additional connections in the OT between the nations and animal imagery. One example is Daniel 7, where the grotesque hybrid beasts are understood to represent various empires. Staples interprets their grotesque image as the result of a "kosher mentality,"[114] suggesting that their unnatural composition reflects their impurity and the mingling of nations. In particular, he draws attention to Daniel 7:5, where the second beast is told to "rise [and] consume much flesh," linking this language to the command in Acts 10:13. He also notes the use of "grotesque beasts to represent empires" in later literature such as *4 Ezra*, the *Testament of Naphtali*, and even Revelation. Staples further connects this with prophetic imagery in Isaiah and Jeremiah—specifically Jeremiah 5:6, which references a wolf, leopard, and lion, as animals depicting nations that would attack Israel—the same pairings found in Isaiah and in the Animal Apocalypse. This repetition, he suggests, signals a kind of established cultural idiom where animals symbolically represent Gentile nations.[115] One more example Staples offers is the portrayal of the Philistines as dogs in the *Animal Apocalypse*—a detail that may shed light on Jesus referring to the Syrophoenician woman as a "dog" in Mark's Gospel.[116]

---

113 Staples, "Animals as Nations," 6–7.

114 Staples, "Animals as Nations," 7. One could speculate on the "mixing" idea stemming from the Law's prohibition of mixing of natural things: seeds, animals, cloths, etc.

115 Staples, "Animals as Nations," 8.

116 Ibid., see his comment on 8n18. Caution and nuancing ought to be taken here, however. It is difficult, if not impossible, for us to imagine Jesus speaking in such a way to one with faith, an attitude that he absolutely does not have elsewhere. I maintain that the

The symmetry in this imagery is telling and may very well explain both the purpose and nature of Peter's vision. When set against the backdrop of Jewish views that regarded Gentiles as defiled, along with the traditions that followed such thinking, a vision drawing from the *Animal Apocalypse* would be a fitting choice on God's part. The sheet, lowered by its four corners, could symbolize the four corners of the earth,[117] naturally invoking language of the ingathering of the nations—an image that would resonate deeply with Peter, a first-century Jew likely familiar with 1 Enoch and the cultural ideas associated

---

whole situation is thematic and polemical, i.e., Jesus knew that it would be recorded and that his present audience would understand what was being said. With the background reference in mind the whole account would center on the dogs getting the scraps from the table, thus further demonstrating (if even implicitly, but to be explicit eventually) the inclusion of Gentiles at God's Table, i.e., part of his family and the covenantal people. For more on the topic of dogs, Gentiles, and the use by Jesus and Paul, see Matthew Thiessen, "Gentiles as Impure Animals in the Writings of Early Christ Followers." Pages 19–32 in Michal Bar-Asher Siegal, Wolfgang Grünstäudl, Matthew Thiessen, eds., *Perceiving the Other in Ancient Judaism and Early Christianity*, WUNT 394 (Tübingen: Mohr Siebeck, 2017); Daniel N. Gullotta, "Among Dogs and Disciples: An Examination of the Story of the Canaanite Woman (Matthew 15:21–28) and the Question of the Gentile Mission within the Matthean Community," *NeoT* 48.2 (2014), 325–340; Mark Nanos, "Paul's Reversal of Jews Calling Gentiles 'Dogs' (Philippians 3:2): 1600 Years of an Ideological Tale Wagging an Exegetical Dog?" *BibInt* 17 (2009), 448–482. These show multiple views.

117 Further symbolism is to be found here as it relates to the altar and its four horns of the Temple, simultaneously adding the connection to animals and animal sacrifices, which would draw from the view of Barret's with *thuson* ("kill/sacrifice") connoting sacrificial language, as well as the four corners of the world from which God would draw Israel and Gentile in the prophets (ex., Isa. 11:12). On the altar and its four horns, Paul Heger sees the altar symbolizing the (throne-)Seat of the Deity upon the entire universe with the four horns symbolizing the four corners of the earth and argues persuasively for his position (*The Three Biblical Altar Laws: Developments in the Sacrificial Cult in Practice and Theology: Political and Economic Background*, BZW 279 [Berlin: De Gruyter, 1999], esp. 207–233).

with it. Such a method of communication from God would not fall on deaf ears or blind eyes, either for Peter or for many Jews of his time. Staples points out that in the *Animal Apocalypse*, all the unclean animals are ultimately transformed into white bulls—a symbolic representation of Gentiles being made clean in the eschatological age. He writes, "Given the typical meaning of animals in visionary literature, the trend toward allegorical interpretation of food laws, and the existence of a stream of apocalyptic thought that looked forward to an eschatological transformation of the nations, it is difficult to imagine an apocalyptically minded Jew who believed the messiah had already come interpreting this vision as about anything but the relationship between Jews and Gentiles." Finally, he adds that "the alleged disconnect between the content and interpretation of Peter's dream seems more the result of modern NT interpreters' over-literalism and difficulties" with apocalyptic and symbolic space of Jews and the early church, in which "what may seem on the surface to refer to animals or food is naturally understood as a reference to nations and peoples."[118]

To my knowledge, Staples's proposals remain unchallenged. When we find primary sources that carry similar elements to our text, those sources should be considered in our interpretation. The *Animal Apocalypse*, especially when considered alongside other OT uses of animal imagery, fits the jugsaw puzzle perfectly. Perhaps most compelling are the possible Messianic allusions it contains, particularly the figure responsible for bringing about the eschatological transformation of all the animals representing the nations.[119] Animals hold significant

---

118 Staples, "Animals as Nations," 11.
119 This is in reference to the "white bull" in 90:37 and surrounding material. See the discussion in Daniel C. Olson, *A New Reading of the Animal Apocalypse of 1 Enoch: 'All Nations Shall be Blessed,'* SVTP 24 (Leiden: Brill, 2013), 26–31.

capacity in the realm of allegory and metaphor, and these "zoological imaginations" were certainly not lost on the early church, especially when it came to ethical comparisons between animal traits and human behavior.[120] Moreover, animals, and the animal kingdom, exist within the broader cosmic realm, which reflected humanity's relationship to God. In other words, the state of the animal kingdom reflects the state of God's kingdom on this earth. This is clearly portrayed in prophetic passages like Isaiah 11:6 and 65:25, where the animals—wolf and lamb, leopard and goat, lion and ox—live together in harmony. The imagery paints a picture of peace and restored cosmic order, implying that the violence seen in the animal kingdom is representative of a larger, broken cosmic order. In the eschatological age—the Messianic age of restoration and peace—such violence and bloodshed will be eradicated, even among the animals. Peace will abound everywhere.

The story of the Bible starts with a cunning serpent (Gen. 3:1), centers on the sheep of Israel (1 Kgs. 22:17; Psa. 78:52; 79:13; 95:7; Ezek. 34:10–31; cf. John 10:2–27), and culminates with the Lion of Judah (Rev. 5:5) and the Lamb of God (John 1:29; cf. Gen. 22:8). Throughout Scripture, Israel is consistently portrayed as the vulnerable "prey," while enemy nations and kings are depicted as "predatory" animals. This symbolic contrast isn't limited to the OT—Jesus himself warns his disciples using similar imagery (e.g., Matt. 10:16). The "jungle" or "wilderness" becomes an allegorical stage for the cosmos, reflecting the condition of human society, and God is portrayed not only as sovereign over this wild realm, but also as the one who will tame it and vindicate his sheep.[121] Jesus extends this sheep motif beyond

120 See Patricia Cox Miller, *In the Eye of the Animal: Zoological Imagination in Ancient Christianity* (Philadelphia: University of Pennsylvania Press, 2018), 42–78.
121 For example, Matthew Michael, "Yahweh, the Animal Tamer: Jungles, Wild Animals and

Israel (Matt. 10:6; 15:24), declaring that he has "other sheep that are not of this fold," adding, "I must bring them also, and they will listen to my voice. So there will be one flock, one Shepherd" (John 10:16)— clearly pointing to Jews and Gentiles being united as a single flock under one Shepherd. Additionally, the Book of Revelation portrays the larger cosmos using vivid zoological imagery, especially through depictions of monstrous and grotesque beasts.[122] A consistent pattern emerges: God's people are portrayed as domesticated animals, while the nations are portrayed as wild beasts, often roaming in the wilderness.

The wilderness is also often portrayed as the area outside of God's presence—an untamed space into which he will bring his salvation. In the eschatological and Messianic chapter of Isaiah 43, the prophet declares: "Remember not the former things, nor consider the things of old. Behold, I am doing a new thing; now it springs forth, do you not perceive it? I will make a way in the wilderness and rivers in the desert. The wild beasts will honor Me, the jackals and the ostriches, for I give water in the wilderness, rivers in the desert, to give drink to My chosen people, the people whom I formed for Myself that they might declare My praise" (Isa. 43:18–21). While some might argue that this passage applies exclusively to Israel, particularly to a restored eschatological Israel, similar imagery throughout the OT prophets applies these elements to the nations as well—pointing toward the restoration of the entire world. The motif of "water in the wilderness" carries deep

---

Yahweh's Sovereignty in the Apocalyptic Space of Daniel 7:1–28," *Scriptura* 119.1 (2020), 1–16.

122 Michael Kuykendall, *Lions, Locusts, and the Lamb: Interpreting Key Images in the Book of Revelation* (Eugene, OR: Wipf & Stock, 2019); see also Koert van Bekkum, Jaap Dekker, Henk van de Kamp, Eric Peels, eds., *Playing with Leviathan: Interpretation and Reception of Monsters from the Biblical World*, TBN 21 (Leiden: Brill, 2017).

soteriological and eschatological significance,[123] and the reference to "jackals" and "ostriches" may symbolically represent Gentiles and the nations.[124] Regardless, the imagery of Israel and the nations being gathered from the "four corners" of the world resonates clearly with the imagery found in Peter's vision.

Gillian Feeley-Harnik adds another point, likening Peter's vision to a prayer—specifically, an "elaboration of the traditional Jewish prayer that God would lift a basket to gather the scattered members of the nation of Israel from the four ends into their own land."[125] She also sees a possible allusion to the story of Noah, suggesting that "Peter's vision brings the world back to the creation that God established after he washed away the first one."[126] This connection to Noah introduces a fascinating typological thread, especially since the ark, which carries clear soteriological overtones (cf. 1 Pet. 3:20–21), can be seen as a symbol of salvation for all who are brought into it. Prior to the flood, humanity was united, and after it, humanity was divided,[127] eventually leading

---

123 See, for example, Frances Klopper, "Aspects of Creation: The Water in the Wilderness Motif in the Psalms and the Prophets," *OTE* 18.2 (2005), 253–264.

124 John Goldingay comments that "The tg apparently makes the worshippers human beings who honor Yhwh for making places habitable by human beings that are currently inhabited only by jackals and ostriches, while Hessler (EvT 25 [1965], p. 362) has the animals standing for the gentiles. But the MT seems to speak of the animal world itself joining in the praise of Yhwh when something new buds, as in 42.10–12 (and cf 55.12–13)—not because they are enjoying the water but because they see what Yhwh has done in bringing down Babylon and restoring Israel" (*A Critical and Exegetical Commentary on Isaiah 40–55*, Vol 1., ICC [London: T&T Clark, 2006], 299). Both ideas fairly overlap.

125 Gillian Feeley-Harnik, *The Lord's Table: The Meaning of Food in Early Judaism and Christianity*, rev. ed. (Washington: Smithsonian Institution Press, 1994), 160; quoting A.D. Nock, *Early Gentile Christianity and Its Hellenistic Background* (New York: Harper and Row, 1964), 54–55.

126 Feeley-Harnik, *The Lord's Table*, 161.

127 By this I mean that after the Flood, and later the events at Babel, humanity was being

to the Jew-Gentile distinction. One might even wonder whether there is deeper significance in the small number of clean animals (two) and the larger number of unclean animals (seven) entering the ark. Now, in Christ—the true ark—all enter as one people, cleansed.

Symbolic interpretations like this one are often difficult and can easily lead to speculation, but what we have explored above shows that the Bible contains a rich zoological matrix of imagery and allusion— particularly in eschatological contexts—that provides a fitting and powerful framework for situating Peter's vision. One may dismiss these connections and arrive at their own interpretations of the vision, but as Henry J. Cadbury rightly observed, "when animals or other objects are mentioned in either a literal or a figurative sense it is natural to inquire what the users' experience of them would testify, rather than what has been transferred to the object by tradition or folklore or proverb."[128] To Peter, a first-century Jew, such imagery would have carried immediate clarity the moment Gentiles sent by God arrived at his door. The long-awaited moment had come: the nations—symbolized by animals— were now joining the flock of Israel.[129]

---

consistently divided into "us" and "them/the other."

128 Henry J. Cadbury, "Animals and Symbolism in Luke: Lexical Notes on Luke-Acts, IX," in *Studies in New Testament and Early Christian Literature: Essays in Honor of Allen P. Wikgren*, ed. David Edward Aune, NovTSup 33 (Leiden: Brill, 1972), 8.

129 Brian James Tipton is a recent advocate for seeing zoomorphological language in the NT as symbolizing the nations. In the Parable of the Mustard Seed (Mark 4:30–32), Tipton sees the birds nesting on the Kingdom's branches as depicting the nations. He rejects the meaning of birds "as birds being birds, and thus not needing extensive comment" but rather "as a representation of all the nations taking refuge within the kingdom of God"—specifically "as a symbolic stand-in for their human counterparts, for gentiles being brought into the kingdom of God" ("Mark's Parabolic Aviary: Reading Mark's Parabolic Birds Ecologically with and against Mark's Jesus." Pages 179–204 in Arthur W. Walker-Jones, Suzanna R. Millar, eds., *Ask the Animals: Developing a Biblical Animal*

THE VISION IN ACTS 10

Again, while such an idea might be lost on our Western minds, it would not have been lost on Peter or the original audience. Contrary to R. L. Solberg's erroneous claim that Peter's vision presents a "false analogy" or "false metaphor" that demands a literal reading,[130] the vision operates within the zoological economy of biblical imagery, motifs, symbolism, and eschatological allusion. This symbolic economy provides the proper exegetical and interpretive setting in which the use of animals *aligns perfectly with the precise message God intends to communicate to Peter.* The connection would not have been lost on Peter and his fellow Jews, effectively communicating precisely what God desired them to understand about the inclusion of their newly welcomed Gentile brothers and sisters.

Without Objection: Conclusion of the Vision

Two aspects of Peter's vision that stand out to the reader are found in verses 20 and 29, and they serve to conclude our analysis. In verse 20, the Spirit repeats the threefold pattern and tells the apostle, "Rise, go down, and accompany them without hesitation, for I have sent them." In verse 29, Peter tells his new Gentile brothers and sisters that, having understood the vision and why he was sent for, "I came

---

Hermeneutic, Semeia Studies 104 [Atlanta: SBL Press, 2024], 188). This fits rather well in the same allegory at play in Peter's vision.

130 R. L. Solberg, *What God Has Made Clean,* 54–55. Solberg's whole quote is: "Third, if the vision about food was solely intended as a metaphor for the Gentiles, Jesus was using a false analogy. He was essentially saying, 'Look, Peter, I realize I'm telling you in this vision that all food is clean, but that's not really true. It's just a metaphor to explain that hanging out with Gentiles is okay now.' God does not use false metaphors." Solberg's view grossly misunderstands the nature of literary devices and especially those used in the Bible. His train-of-thought here is peculiar, and he provides no substantiation or explanation for his position and how it resolves similar vision and imagery use in the bible, as discussed above.

without objection." Then, after hearing Cornelius's account of his own vision, Peter declares in verses 34–35, "Truly I understand that God shows no partiality, but in every nation anyone who fears him and does what is right is acceptable to him." What follows is a mini-sermon recounting Israel's salvation history and proclaiming the Gospel in Christ—until Peter is beautifully interrupted by the Spirit falling upon the Gentiles. This moment (1) marks a mini-Pentecost for these Gentiles,[131] (2) infuses the event with eschatological significance, and (3) confirms Peter's unfolding eschatological understanding of what is happening before his eyes. Here, yet another threefold pattern emerges: Peter responds without hesitation, recognizes Cornelius as a symbol of Gentile salvation, and witnesses the Spirit fall upon them— the very same sign that the Jewish believers received.

The words translated as "without hesitation" and "without objection" in Acts 10—*diakrinomenos* and *anantirētōs*, respectively—are connected to the phrase in verse 34, "respecter of persons" (*prosōpolēmptēs*), creating a web of language around the idea of partiality. Although *anantirētōs* can be understood in a neutral sense as "without raising any objection,"[132] in Acts 19:36 it is used adjectively to describe someone responding without rashness, pointing us back to the Spirit's command to Peter to accompany Cornelius's men *diakrinomenos*—"without hesitation" or "without distinction" (Acts 10:20). While *diakrinomenos* can also carry the general meaning of distinguishing or judging,[133] in

---

131 Many note this detail. Just as the Jews awaited the falling of the Holy Spirit, in line with eschatological expectations, so too are these Gentiles receiving him.

132 BDAG, 69.

133 *BDAG* (231) lists six options: "(1) to differentiate by separating, separate, arrange; (2) to conclude that there is a difference, make a distinction, differentiate, (3) to evaluate by paying careful attention to, evaluate, judge, (4) to render a legal decision, judge, decide, (5) to be at variance w. someone, (6) to be uncertain, to be at odds w. oneself, doubt,

this context, it more accurately reflects ethnic discrimination—Peter's internal struggle to avoid Gentiles by "making a distinction" between them and Jews.[134] This interpretation is reinforced at the Jerusalem Council, where Peter says, "Brothers, you know that in the early days God made a choice among you, that by my mouth the Gentiles should hear the word of the gospel and believe. And God, who knows the heart, bore witness to them, by giving them the Holy Spirit just as he did to us, and he made no distinction (*diekrinen*) between us and them, having cleansed their hearts by faith" (Acts 15:7–9). Note especially that the word *diekrinen* is the aorist, active, indicative form of the same verb found in Acts 10:20 and 11:12.

Additionally, Peter makes no mention whatsoever of animals being cleansed when he recounts the vision in chapter 11—remarkably so, considering the common claim that the vision is about the abrogation of the dietary laws. Instead, he emphasizes that God "cleansed" (*katharisas*; cf. 10:15 *ekatharise*) the hearts of the Gentiles. Furthermore, the circumcision party "criticized" (*diekrinonto*) Peter for entering the home of uncircumcised Gentiles (Acts 11:2–3), using a word that may intentionally echo and even ironically reflect the same "making distinctions" (*diakrinomenos*) Peter was commanded by the Spirit not to make. This repetition—occurring three times, notably—grounds the entire situation within the larger theme of ethnic distinction and partiality, which the vision directly addresses. The message is unmistakable: Gentiles are not to be discriminated against or avoided, for God shows no partiality. Rather, as Peter says, "in every nation" (*en panti ethnei*, Acts 10:35), anyone who fears God and does what is right is acceptable to him.

---

waver." They take 10:20 here under (6), "hesitate."

134 See the discussion in Eschner, "Purity and Impurity of Food and People," 381–385.

It is unfathomable that Peter, speaking at the Jerusalem Council regarding what is required of Gentiles, would fail to mention the supposed cleansing of unclean animals—especially if that were the primary takeaway from his vision.[135] For us, this omission should serve as the final nail in the coffin of the antinomian interpretation. Notably, Paul himself never once appeals to Peter's vision in his arguments about the Law, further reinforcing this point. What we have in Acts 10 is not a statement on food laws but a beautiful, symbolic vision designed to tear down the borders of ethnic distinction and Jewish exclusivity. It is a divine revelation to Peter that God has purified all who come to him in faith, that he is not a respecter of persons, and that Peter is no longer to differentiate between Jew and Gentile—between insiders and outsiders—for all are truly one in Christ through faith. *This* is the meaning of Acts 10.

Based on all the observations made above, we can now draw the following conclusions regarding a proper interpretation of Peter's vision and its implications:

1. From Peter's initial reception and understanding of the vision, to his explanation of it to his fellow Jews—and even throughout later patristic interpretation—there is no indication that the vision referred to the cleansing of unclean animals or the

---

135 Eschner ("Purity and Impurity of Food and People," 380–381) comments that in Acts 11, "First, Peter in his defense," if the Jews' rebuke of him was eating unkosher foodstuff, "could have reasoned that Cornelius never served any food forbidden to Jews, which seems likely given his characterization as 'just' and 'pious.' Secondly, Peter could argue that Jewish Christians and therefore he himself no longer have to obey the Jewish dietary laws. However, the text at hand does not suggest that Peter indeed violated the food laws." His silence would strongly suggest that Acts 15 is not about the Law's abrogation for Gentiles, either.

annulment of the food laws. Such a conclusion is instead a later interpolation without any textual basis. Peter himself clearly presents the interpretation as being strictly and exclusively about *people*.

2. The lexical and historical distinction between the terms "unclean" and "common," along with the preferable textual reading of the disjunctive "or" rather than "and," clarifies the meaning of the vision with respect to Jewish perceptions of Gentiles as "defiled" and addresses the issue of hesitancy surrounding Jew-Gentile table-fellowship. This more accurate reading also makes the interpretation that God "cleansed" the intrinsically "unclean" untenable, as the text indicates that his cleansing pertains to the "common." God's action, then, is the purifying of those considered defiled and defiling, *not* the cleansing of what is intrinsically unclean.

3. Given the zoological language and allegory found throughout the OT and Second Temple Period literature, the use of animals in Peter's vision serves to symbolize the various nations (Gentiles) of the world. It reinforces the concept of being "common by association" and places the vision within the eschatological-apocalyptic domain, in which all nations and peoples are gathered to God and regarded as equal. The animals thus represent both Israel and the nations being brought together into a single vessel (the sheet) from the four corners of the earth.

4. When Peter's vision is viewed within its larger contextual setting, the interpretation that it concerns food being cleansed appears foreign and forced, lacking and any clear foundation for its abrupt insertion into the narrative. The literary elements present—particularly the threefold pattern—direct the reader

to conclude that people, as the central focus of the narrative, are the objects symbolized by the vision. Other narrative elements, such as the parallels with Jonah, Peter, Dorcas, etc., further support this interpretation.

5. The fact that Peter shows no recollection of a supposed food-cleansing event in Mark 7 casts serious doubt on such an interpretation, and the presence of the term "common" further suggests that reading it as a reference to food law abrogation is entirely interpolative.

While additional points could be addressed, the five outlined above are sufficient for our purposes. From both a simple and close reading of Peter's vision in Acts 10, along with its surrounding context in Acts 9:36–11:18 and the broader narrative of Acts as a whole, there is no exegetical basis for interpreting the passage as referring to the cleansing of animals or the abrogation of dietary regulations with any textual consistency. Instead, the vision's multifaceted nature centers on an eschatological-apocalyptic revelation concerning the "cleansing" of the nations—now counted among God's redeemed and purified people—fulfilling the prophetic and often allegorical expectations found throughout the Scriptures and Jewish literature. The extent to which the vision relates to food appears limited to the issue of Jewish purity traditions and previously held (but now overturned) perceptions of intrinsic Gentile impurity that prevented table-fellowship. Andrew McGowan offers a helpful summary of both the interpretive context and broader implications of the vision:

> While divine command had proclaimed a lack of distinction
> between animals, the explicit zoomorphic interpretation of

the vision leaves the conclusions to be drawn about actual diet unclear...If the story of Peter and Cornelius is about commensality rather than diet, we should certainly balk at the common but tendentious scholarly conclusion that the story of Peter and Cornelius is a 'clear and blunt reversal of Jewish food laws.' This is to confuse (under all-too-typical supersessionist interpretive assumptions) the metaphorical frame of the vision with its ethical application. The explicit interpretation of the vision has nothing to do with food laws. While the interpretive strands presented here, of allegory and zoomorphy, on the one hand, and synecdoche, on the other, do involve renegotiation of commensality and perhaps hence ultimately of diet itself, the question of diet is raised only implicitly, and not answered...While the animals in the vision story of Acts 10 seem initially to be actors or agents in a story, they turn out to be virtual animals, mere signs of different things, of people in fact. Real animals make only an implied appearance there, under the guise of commensality, which may have meant consumption of animal flesh. For this reason among others, the scholarly overreading of that story as representing some sort of abrogation of the Mosaic law is fanciful at best.[136]

---

136 Andrew McGowan, "Animal Acts: Diet and Law in the Acts of the Apostles," in *Animals and the Law in Antiquity*, ed. Saul M. Olyan and Jordan D. Rosenblum, *BJS* 368 (Providence, RI: Brown University, 2021), 112–3, 117–8. In-text quote from Eldon Jay Epp, "Early Christian Attitudes" (2016), 153.

CHAPTER 3
WHOM GOD HAS MADE CLEAN

The Bible is like a tapestry, woven through layers of intertextual allusions, recurring themes, motifs, and literary elements that connect its various parts into an organic, cohesive whole. At the center of this tapestry emerges the Image of Christ—the *telos* of human history—toward whom everything anticipates, to whom everything points, and in whom everything finds its end. Yet the Bible is also a story—a narrative of creation, fall, and the journey to the Cross. With each miracle, covenant, event, and act, we see new chapters unfolding on the stage of God's great story. Acts 10 fits seamlessly into this larger narrative. Within this enigmatic vision, framed by the broader theme of God's reconciling work in Acts, another step in the restoration of creation unfolds before Peter's eyes: the inclusion of the nations into the people of God, restored with Israel. Set firmly within the developing narrative of the Gospel's expansion to the ends of the earth, Peter's vision marks the moment he personally witnesses the reality of a new era—one in which lineage no longer defines belonging, but cleansing through faith in Christ does. Rather than signaling some ambiguous abrogation of dietary laws, the vision offers something far more beautiful and profound. It is not about liberty over diet, but the spiritual liberty now available to all who come to God in faith.

Modern-day Christians often take too simplistic an approach to the Bible—a reading restricted to a "chapter and verse" type of framework and fails to take into consideration the multiple elements potentially at play. This has the potential to make God's Word superficial, and to miss the forest for the trees. Scripture weaves through layers of themes, imagery, and allegory, spinning a web that presents an intricate image—one that calls for close attentiveness to its organic whole. The Bible invites—indeed, demands—its readers to fully immerse in its symbolic and literary world, putting together the various pieces like a beautiful, though often complex, picture. In this regard, "The Bible shares the mentality of the ancient Near East," emerging from that world. "Every student of the Bible knows that certain expressions are not to be understood 'literally.' But it is not at all easy, given specific instances, to follow the peculiarities of ancient Near Eastern thought."[1] While this symbolic and layered mode of communication may feel foreign to modern readers, the NT continues a long literary tradition shaped over centuries by the cultural environments in which it was formed. These details often challenge our modern interpretive sensibilities, but the Bible does not play by our rules or self-imposed frameworks.

What our text at hand—the vision in Acts 10—presents is a "play" of Peter's Jewish ancestry and the symbolic world in which he was raised. For Peter, the meaning and the vehicle through which it was conveyed would have felt familiar and natural. On the other side of history, we often fail to appreciate this, but such is the struggle of interpreting the Bible: it was written *for* us, but not *to* us.[2] Our job is to place ourselves in the first century imagination as much as we can in order to receive it as it was originally given.

Beyond the obvious textual evidence that the vision includes no suggestion of a dual interpretation, the literary background establishes a symbolic world for Peter's interpretation. In this book, we have

---

1 Othmar Keel, *The Symbolism of the Biblical World: Ancient Near Eastern Iconography and the Book of Psalms* (Winona Lake, IN: Eisenbrauns, 1997), 9. See the brief overview of the depiction of animals as enemies in 85–88.

2 This is a popular saying by OT scholar John H. Walton.

traced the textual evidence—what may be called the "plain interpretive approach"—and complemented its "surface meaning" with "symbolic elucidation" drawn from Israel's traditional literature. The way Enoch's *Animal Apocalypse* serves as a symbolic background for the theology of Acts cannot go unappreciated. It seems every detail finds its place: set within the Jew-Gentile dichotomy and framed in the realized eschatological, Messianic age, the two groups are portrayed as animals— fully consistent with Jewish literary tradition—as God challenges and dismantles Peter's traditional distinction between his people and the "Other." That the *Animal Apocalypse* ends with ethnic borders dissolved and all the animals—both Jews and the nations—being transformed into a type of "new creation" through the one White Bull perfectly mirrors the NT's own new creation soteriology, where ethnicity becomes an irrelevant construct of the old age. In Christ, each believer is a new creation (2 Cor. 5:17).[3]

In Peter's vision, the Gentiles are portrayed not only as unclean animals, but dangerous ones as well. The Hebrew Bible often depicted these animals as hostile nations, and the association of these animals with Gentiles seen as threats would linger in Peter's mind. But Peter learns that these Gentiles are not to be seen as threats—God has already subdued the dangerous and is calling in those from the wilderness. Peter is now to do the same. He is a shepherd, not a hunter. The question is: does he love Christ's sheep? The Vision echoes, in a way, Jesus's original questions to Peter in John 21:15–17, and perhaps even the call to "feed" Christ's sheep is alluded to here. After all, one cannot feed people, whether literally or spiritually, without first being willing to associate with them. Though there are still wolves, dogs, and serpents in the wilderness, Peter's mission is to seek the sheep from

---

3   See Michael E. Fuller's discussion in *The Restoration of Israel*, 60–74.

other folds. God has prepared him for this very calling. Set within the biblical tradition of the nations being depicted as wild animals and God as the one who tames them, ultimately forming one flock under one Shepherd, the beauty of the vision is tragically missed by many modern readers. It is not about *what* God has made clean, but *whom* God has made clean.

Other than the main element of the vision involving animals, several additional details reinforce its clear and intended meaning. Acts 10 is preceded by imagery suggestive of animals and prophetic wilderness restoration through the figure of Dorcas, and is also certainly grounded in allusions to the prophet Jonah—both of which prepare the reader thematically for what follows. Immediately after the vision, three men arrive at Peter's door, and the Spirit gives a unique threefold command: "Rise, go down, and accompany"—a direct literary parallel of the earlier "Rise, kill, and eat." This threefold pattern is no coincidence but serves as a signaling literary device, pointing the reader toward the proper interpretation. Additionally, when we consider the contextual distinctions between "unclean" and "common" in first-century Judaism, along with a more grammatically precise understanding of what God is actually "cleansing" in the vision, we begin to see the act depicted for what it is: a divine illustration of inclusion—not of animals, but of people. Finally, the plainness of Peter's own interpretation—that the vision pertains to people and not animals—is the icing on our exegetical cake. From every perspective—textual, grammatical, theological—a dual-interpretation fails. In the end, we ought to just take Peter at his own word.

Instead of approaching Peter's vision with the baggage of dogmatic commitments or entrenched theological assumptions, this book has aimed to take a simple and pragmatic approach, using relevant background information to color in the lines of what might otherwise appear ambiguous. While it would be easy to extend the discussion into a full-fledged monologue by exploring every possible detail, what has been presented should be sufficient to cast serious doubt on the typical, antinomian interpretation. Based on our semantic, contextual, cultural, and literary investigation, it is difficult—if not impossible—to defend the idea that Peter's vision depicts anything other than the cleansing of Gentiles.

Implications for Other Passages

The fact that Acts 10 cannot be reasonably presented as signaling the discontinuity of the Law holds significant implications for how we approach other passages in Scripture. As a passage often treated as a cornerstone argument against the Law's continued relevance for the Church, our investigation invites us to reconsider how we have interpreted other disputed passages. While many of those have not been addressed in this book, that was never the intent, and they will be given their own focused attention in the *Pronomian Pocket Guide* series. For now, we are left to ask a simple question: what now? Perhaps a good starting point is this: maybe we have imposed modern ethical and moral concerns onto passages that are, in reality, grounded in salvation-historical developments. Like Acts 10, we must examine the first-century context and re-evaluate our interpretations accordingly. When a passage speaks of the Law, is it truly addressing the Law itself? Or is it dealing with the pressing issue of conversion to Judaism as a prerequisite for belonging to God's people? And when provisions for table fellowship are introduced, as in Acts 15, does that necessarily imply the annulment of the Law as a whole—or is the Law even the subject at all? If Peter was so entangled in Jewish traditions that forbade association with people of other nations, might passages like

Mark 7, Acts 15, and Romans 14 also be addressing similar concerns rather than abolishing the Law?

The need to reconsider other passages of Scripture becomes all the more weighty when we recognize that Acts 10 does not follow the assumed pattern of the Law's abrogation. In effect, what we have done is break a link in that supposed chain—an act that justifies further investigation into whether the entire chain may, in fact, be a fabrication of interpolation. Once we are willing to lay aside our presuppositions and the traditional interpretations we have inherited, an entirely new perspective begins to take shape. With this fresh lens, we are freed to approach the Scriptures in a way that is both proper and contextually grounded. As we mentioned in chapter 1, all of us are susceptible to assumptions and traditions that slant our readings, no matter the topic or doctrine under consideration. The first step in becoming honest, objective, and diligent students of God's Word is to ask ourselves whether we've misunderstood or misread certain passages. If we cannot be wrong, we can never be right.

The NT is not concerned with liberating Christians from the supposed oppressive chains of the Law. True spiritual liberty is not freedom *from* righteousness, but freedom *into* righteousness. The eschatological vision of the Messianic age envisioned a time when God's people would be able to keep the Law, not abandon it altogether. This is the vision behind passages like Jeremiah 31 and Ezekiel 36. The Law is not the problem; *sin* is the problem, along with humanity's inability and unwillingness to obey the Law. A Law-less Gospel fails to image the OT's expectation of humanity's restoration. What the NT is actually concerned with is the inbreaking of the Gospel into the cosmos, proclaiming deliverance from the flesh and from sin through Christ to all people everywhere. It is accompanied by the giving of the Holy Spirit, who enables us to keep the Law. Seeking to keep the Law is not an attempt to "add to the finished work of Christ." Far from it. Nothing can save apart from grace and faith in the Living Savior. Rather, in Christ, we are newly created for good works (Eph. 2:10).

Too frequently, we approach the Bible as if it were written directly and specifically for us. And while it certainly does apply to us, we are not its immediate audience—we are recipients of it second-hand. The Bible's message is intended for all people in all times, as the Gospel is the universal message of salvation. However, the way that message was first delivered came through very particular means: the NT was written in a specific historical moment, dealing with specific issues, and within specific cultural, social, and religious frameworks very different from our own. To be sure, the Gospel was not merely a message about individual salvation from sin—it was the dramatic inbreaking of the God of Israel into the world of the nations, bringing with it the announcement of spiritual truth for all. Put simply, the NT was written in a highly polemical environment, often featuring Jews arguing with other Jews, while also explaining to Gentiles how they too could now share in the salvation found in Christ. This core theological context is vital for understanding the NT, yet it is far too often neglected.

Just as we have seen that Peter's vision in Acts 10 should be understood as a moment of prophetic fulfillment and a key event in salvation history—rather than an abrogation of the Law—we must now ask whether other pericopes follow the same pattern. What we will soon find is that nearly every debated passage concerning the Law and salvation is less about *how* one is saved and more about *who* is saved. The bogeyman caricature of the first-century Jew as a legalist obsessed with works-based salvation has not hindered Jewish-Christian relations, but it also continues to distort our readings of Scripture with anachronistic and inaccurate assumptions. In a time when knowledge and resources are more accessible than ever before, my prayer is that we be inspired—like children—to remain curious, to ask honest questions, and to investigate, no matter what we have been taught, heard, or grown up believing. Because if Acts 10 has been so misunderstood for so long, we have to ask: what about other passages?

Concluding Remarks

While the belief that the Law holds no relevance for the modern believer will continue, it is my hope that this work represents a step forward in challenging and ultimately overturning that view within the Church. I also hope that the arguments presented here prove compelling enough to be thoughtfully considered, adopted, and accepted, particularly in helping to realign our reading of Acts 10 with its proper contextual environment. More than that, however, my greater hope is that this work inspires readers to dig deeper into the Bible and its world. Scripture presents us with a sea of knowledge, endless in breadth and immeasurable in depth, and while we will never reach its end, or explore its vastness, we always enjoy and seek to wade in its waters. And in doing so, may we come to recognize the importance of reading it not simply as we receive it, but as it was originally given.

There is always more to the text than initially meets the eye, and this is something we encounter in any given passage. Often, the theological depth and richness contained within are so profound that to reduce a passage—such as interpreting Acts 10 as annulling food laws—feels like a disservice. While God's Word certainly deals with the practical, the commanded, and even the mundane, approaching it first and foremost as the unfolding revelation of God's plan to reconcile his fallen creation to himself brings lasting reward—not only in our study, but in our lives as we become another actor within this grand story of salvation. If we seek first the Kingdom of God, setting aside our own wills, opinions, and desires, the rest will fall quite into place.

POSTSCRIPT

The Law and its application to the believer is a dense topic—one that naturally draws from every area of theology and biblical studies. My prayer is that this treatment of Acts 10 has proven to be a meaningful and worthwhile read for you, the reader, and that it stands as a valuable contribution to the promising series by Pronomian Publishing. A topic of this magnitude requires many voices and many volumes to capture its full breadth, and this series is committed to meeting that need.

For those interested in following more of my journey as I explore the Scriptures and share insights for fellow curious seekers, I invite you to visit my website at www.olychnos.com, where I blog, review books, and post updates on published work. I also oversee *The Engrafted Word Ministry*, a Messianic teaching and outreach ministry serving the homeless. We are on Facebook (@theengraftedword), and more information is available on our website: www.theengraftedwordministry.com.

May HaShem bless and keep you,

Rick

BIBLIOGRAPHY

Allen, Lesie C. *The Books of Joel, Obadiah, Jonah, and Micah*. New International Commentary on the Old Testament. Grand Rapids, MI: Eerdmans, 1976.

Anderson, Joel E. "Jonah in Mark and Matthew: Creation, Covenant, Christ, and the Kingdom of God." *Biblical Theology Bulletin* 42.4 (2012): 172–186.

Averbeck, Richard E. *The Old Testament Law for the Life of the Church: Reading the Torah in the Light of Christ*. Downers Grove, IL: IVP Academic, 2022.

Bailey, R. M. *Neither Circumcision Nor Uncircumcision: A Messianic and Exegetical Commentary on the Book of Galatians*. Independently Published, 2023.

Banks, Robert. "Matthew's Understanding of the Law: Authenticity and Interpretation in Matthew 5:17–20." *Journal of Biblical Literature* 93.2 (1974): 226–262.

Barclay, John M. G. *Paul and the Power of Grace*. Grand Rapids, MI: Eerdmans, 2020.

Barrett, C. K. *Acts 1–14*. International Critical Commentary. Two Volumes. Edinburgh: T&T Clark, 2004.

Bartolomew, Craig G., Ryan P. O'Dowd. *Old Testament Wisdom Literature: A Theological Introduction*. Downers Grove, IL: IVP Academic, 2011.

Beale, G. K. *The Temple and the Church's Mission: A Biblical Theology of the Dwelling Place of God*. New Studies in Biblical Theology 17. Downers Grove, IL: IVP Academic, 2004.

Beale, G. K. "The Descent of the Eschatological Temple in the Form of the Spirit at Pentecost." Two Parts: "The Clearest Evidence" and "Corroborating Evidence." *Tyndale Bulletin* 56.1 (2005): 73–102 / 56.2 (2005): 63–90.

Bibb, Bryan D. *Ritual Words and Narrative Worlds in the Book of Leviticus.* Edinburgh: T&T Clark, 2008.

Bickerman, Elias J. "A Seleucid Proclamation Concerning the Temple in Jerusalem" in *Studies in Jewish and Christian History: Ancient Judaism and Early Christianity* 68. Volume 1. Leiden: Brill, 2007.

Bird, Michael F. *Crossing Over Sea and Land: Jewish Missionary Activity in the Second Temple Period.* Grand Rapids, MI: Baker Academic, 2010.

Block, Daniel I. "Deuteronomy." Pages 67–82 in Kevin J. Vanhoozer, ed., *Theological Interpretation of the Old Testament: A Book-by-Book Survey.* Grand Rapids, MI: Baker Academic, 2008.

Bock, Darrel L. *Acts.* Baker Exegetical Commentary on the New Testament. Grand Rapids, MI: Baker Academic, 2007.

Booth, Roger P. *Jesus and the Laws of Purity: Tradition History and Legal History in Mark 7.* Journal for the Study of the New Testament Supplement Series 13. Sheffield: Sheffield Academic Press, 1986.

Boström, Lennart. "Retribution and Wisdom Literature." Pages 134–154 in David G. Firth, Lindsay Wilson, eds., *Interpreting Old Testament Wisdom Literature.* Downers Grove, IL: IVP Academic, 2017.

Boyarin, Daniel. *The Jewish Gospels: The Story of the Jewish Christ.* New York: The New Press, 2012.

Boyarin, Daniel. "An Isogloss in First-Century Jewry: Josephus and Mark on the Purpose of the Law." Pages 63–81 in Michal Bar-Asher Siegal, Tzvi Novick, Christine Hayes, eds., *The Faces of*

Torah: Studies in the Texts and Contexts of Ancient Judaism in Honor of Steven Fraade. Göttingen: V&R Academic, 2017.

Brink, Laurie. *Soldiers in Luke-Acts: Engaging, Contradicting, and Transcending the Stereotypes.* Wissenschaftliche Untersuchungen zum Neuen Testament 362. Tübingen: Mohr Siebeck, 2014.

Bruce, F. F. *The Book of Acts.* New International Commentary on the New Testament. Revised Edition. Grand Rapids, MI: Eerdmans, 1988.

Cadbury, Henry J. "Animals and Symbolism in Luke: Lexical Notes on Luke-Acts, IX." Pages 3–15 in David Edward Aune, ed., *Studies in New Testament and Early Christian Literature: Essays in Honor of Allen P. Wikgren.* Novum Testamentum Supplement Series 33. Leiden: Brill, 1972.

Cusimano, Jeremy. "Study Finds Land Fallowing Improves Soil Quality in PVID." University of Arizona. *Water Resource Quarterly* 22.1 (2014): 1-4.

Cohen, Shaye J. D. "Crossing the Boundary and Becoming a Jew." *Harvard Theological Review* 82.1 (1989): 13-33.

Collins, John J. "The Transformation of the Torah in Second Temple Judaism." *Journal for the Study of Judaism* 45.4 (2012): 455–474.

Collins, John J. *The Invention of Judaism: Torah and Jewish Identity from Deuteronomy to Paul.* Berkeley: University of California Press, 2017.

Collman, Ryan D. *The Apostle to the Foreskin: Circumcision in the Letters of Paul.* Beihefte zur Zeitschrift für die Alttestamentliche Wissenschaft 259. Boston: Berlin: De Gruyter, 2023.

Crossley, James G. *The Date of Mark's Gospel: Insight from the Law in Earliest Christianity.* Journal for the Study of the New Testament Supplement Series 266. New York: T&T Clark, 2004.

Davies, W. D. *Paul and Rabbinic Judaism: Some Rabbinic Elements in Pauline Theology*. Minneapolis: Fortress Press, 1980.

den Hejier, Arco. *Portraits of Paul's Performance in the Book of Acts: Luke's Apologetic Strategy in the Depiction of Paul as a Messenger of God*. Wissenschaftliche Untersuchungen zum Neuen Testament 556. Tübingen: Mohr Siebeck, 2021.

Dunn, James D. G. *The Acts of the Apostles*. Grand Rapids, MI: Eerdmans, 1996.

Dunn, James D. G. *The Theology of Paul the Apostle*. Grand Rapids, MI: Eerdmans, 2006.

Dunn, James D. G. *The Epistle to the Galatians*. Black's New Testament Commentary. Peabody, MA: Hendrickson Publishers, 2006.

Doole, J. Andrew. *What was Mark for Matthew? An Examination of Matthew's Relationship and Attitude to His Primacy Source*. Wissenschaftliche Untersuchungen zum Neuen Testament 344. Tübingen: Mohr Siebeck, 2013.

Eschner, Christina. "Purity and Impurity of Food and People in Acts 10:1–11:18: Is the Abolition of Jewish Food Laws at the Center of the Cornelian Narrative?" Pages 359–394 in Lutz Doering, Jörg Frey, Laura von Bartenwerffer, eds., *Purity in Ancient Judaism: Texts, Contexts, and Concepts*. Wissenschaftliche Untersuchungen zum Neuen Testament 528. Tübingen, Mohr Siebeck, 2025.

Feder, Yitzhaq. "The Semantics of Purity in the Ancient Near East: Lexical Meaning as a Projection of Embodied Existence." *Journal of Ancient Near Eastern Religions* 14 (2014): 87-113.

Feder, Yitzhaq. "Defilement, Disgust, and Disease: The Experiential Basis of Hittite and Akkadian Terms for Iniquity." *Journal of the American Oriental Society* 136.1 (2016): 99-116.

Feeley-Harnik, Gillian. *The Lord's Table: The Meaning of Food in Early Judaism and Christianity*. Rev. ed. Washington: Smithsonian Institution Press, 1994.

Feldman, Louis J. "Conversion to Judaism in Classical Antiquity." *Hebrew Union College Annual* 74 (2003): 115–156.

Fitzmeyer, Joseph A. *The Acts of the Apostles: A New Translation with Introduction and Commentary*. Anchor Yale Bible Commentary 31. New York: Doubleday, 1998.

Fitzpatrick-McKinley, Anne. *The Transformation of Torah from Scribal Advice to Law*. Library of Hebrew Bible and Old Testament Studies 287. Sheffield: Sheffield Academic Press, 1999.

France, R. T. *The Gospel of Matthew*. New International Commentary of the New Testament. Grand Rapids, MI: Eerdmans, 2007.

Friedberg, Albert D. *Crafting the 613 Commandments: Maimonides on the Enumeration, Classification and Formulation of the Scriptural Commandments*. Boston: Academic Studies Press, 2013.

Fuller, Michael E. *The Restoration of Israel: Israel's Re-Gathering and the Fate of the Nations in Early Jewish Literature and Luke-Acts*. Beihefte zur Zeitschrift für die alttestamentliche Wissenschaft 138. Boston: Berlin: De Gruyter, 2006.

Furstenberg, Yair. "Defilement Penetrating the Body: A New Understanding of Contamination in Mark 7:15." *New Testament Studies* 54 (2008): 176–200.

Garlington, Don G. "The Obedience of Faith": A Pauline Phrase in Historical Context. PhD diss., University of Durham, 1987.

Goldingay, John. *A Critical and Exegetical Commentary on Isaiah 40–55*. Volume One. International Critical Commentary. London: T&T Clark, 2006.

Gordon, Benjamin D. *Land and Temple: Field Sacralization and the Agrarian Priesthood of Second Temple Judaism.* Studia Judaica 87. Berlin: Boston: De Gruyter, 2020.

Gullotta, Daniel N. "Among Dogs and Disciples: An Examination of the Story of the Canaanite Woman (Matthew 15:21–28) and the Question of the Gentile Mission within the Matthean Community." *Neotestamentica* 48.2 (2014): 325–340.

Gundry, Robert H. *Mark: A Commentary on His Apology for the Cross.* Grand Rapids, MI: Eerdmans, 1993.

Hackett, Horatio B. *A Commentary on the Original Text of the Acts of the Apostles.* Revised Edition. Boston: Gould & Lincoln, 1858.

Hagner, Donald. *How New is the New Testament? First-Century Judaism and the Emergence of Christianity.* Grand Rapids, MI: Baker Academic, 2018.

Heger, Paul. *The Three Biblical Altar Laws: Developments in the Sacrificial Cult in Practice and Theology: Political and Economic Background.* Beihefte zur Zeitschrift für die alttestamentliche Wissenschaft 279. Berlin: De Gruyter, 1999.

Henderson, Ian H. *Jesus, Rhetoric and Law.* Biblical Interpretation Series 20. Leiden: Brill, 1996.

Holloday, William L. *Concise Hebrew and Aramaic Lexicon of the Old Testament.* Grand Rapids, MI: Eerdmans, 1988.

House, Colin. "Defilement by Association: Some Insights from the Usage of ΚΟΙΝΌ/ΚΟΙΝΌΩ in Acts 10 and 11." *Andrews University Seminary Studies* 21.2 (1985): 143–153.

Humphrey, E. M. "Collisions of Modes? Vision and Determining Argument in Acts 10:1–11:18." *Semeia* 71 (1995): 65–84.

Jobes, Karen H. *1, 2, and 3 John.* Zondervan Exegetical Commentary of the New Testament. Grand Rapids, MI: Zondervan Academic, 2014.

Kaiser Jr., Walter J. *Mission in the Old Testament: Israel as a Light to the Nations*. Second Edition. Grand Rapids, MI: Baker Academic, 2012.

Kazen, Thomas. *Issues of Impurity in Early Judaism*. Itero 4. Stockholm: Enskila Högskolan Stockholm, 2021.

Keel, Othmar. *The Symbolism of the Biblical World: Ancient Near Eastern Iconography and the Book of Psalms*. Winona Lake, IN: Eisenbrauns, 1997.

Keener, Craig S. *Acts: An Exegetical Commentary*. Four Volumes. Grand Rapids, MI: Baker Academic, 2013.

Keener, Craig S. *The IVP Bible Background Commentary: New Testament*. Second Edition. Downers Grove, IL: IVP Academic, 2014.

Kellum, L. Scott. *Acts. Exegetical Guide to the Greek New Testament*. Nashville, TN: B&H Academic, 2020.

Klawans, Jonathan. *Impurity and Sin in Ancient Judaism*. Oxford: Oxford University Press, 2000.

Klingbeil Gerald A. "Altars, Ritual and Theology: Preliminary Thoughts on the Importance of Cult and Ritual for a Theology of the Hebrew Scriptures." *Vestus Testamentum* 54.4 (2004): 495–515.

Klopper, Frances. "Aspects of Creation: The Water in the Wilderness Motif in the Psalms and the Prophets." *Old Testament Essays* 18.2 (2005): 253–264.

Konradt, Matthias. *The Gospel According to Matthew: A Commentary*. Translated by M. Eugene Boring. Waco, TX: Baylor University Press, 2020.

Kramer, Ross S. "Giving up the Godfearers." *Journal of Ancient Judaism* 5.1 (2014): 61–87.

Kruger, Thomas. *Qoheleth: A Commentary on the Book of Qoheleth*. Hermenia. Augsburg: Fortress Press, 2004.

Kruse, Colin G. *The Letters of John*. Pillar New Testament Commentary. Grand Rapids, MI: Eerdmans, 2020.

Kuykendall, Michael. *Lions, Locusts, and the Lamb: Interpreting Key Images in the Book of Revelation*. Eugene, OR: Wipf & Stock, 2019.

Kwon, JiSeong J. Seth A. Bledsoe, eds., *Between Wisdom and Torah: Discourses on Wisdom and Law in Second Temple Judaism*. Deuterocanonical and Canonical Literature 51. Berlin: De Gruyter, 2023.

Kyrychenko, Alexander. *The Roman Army and the Expansion of the Gospel: The Role of the Centurion in Luke-Acts*. Beihefte zur Zeitschrift für die alttestamentliche Wissenschaft 203. Boston: De Gruyter, 2014.

LeFebvre, Michael. *Collections, Codes, and Torah: The Re-Characterization of Israel's Written Law*. Library of Hebrew Bible and Old Testament Studies 451. New York: T&T Clark, 2006.

Leichman, Abigail Klein. "SHMITA: The Israeli Farmers Who Are Giving Their Land a Year's Rest - Jewish Ledger." *Jewish Ledger*, 3 Sept. 2021, www. jewishledger.com/2021/09/shmita-the-israeli-farmers-who-are-giving-their-land-a-years-rest.

Levinskaya, Irina. *The Book of Acts in Its Diaspora Setting*. Book of Acts in its First Century Setting 5. Grand Rapids, MI: Eerdmans, 1996.

Liggins, Stephen S. *Many Convincing Proofs: Persuasive Phenomena Associated with Gospel Proclamation in Acts*. Beihefte zur Zeitschrift für die alttestamentliche Wissenschaft 221. Berlin: Boston: De Gruyter, 2016.

Lloyd, J. A. *Archaeology and the Itinerant Jesus: A Historical Enquiry into Jesus' Itinerant Ministry in the North*. Wissenschaftliche Untersuchungen zum Neuen Testament 564. Tübingen: Mohr Siebeck, 2022.

Luz, Ulrich. *Matthew 1–7*. Hermenia. Augsburg: Fortress Press, 2007.

Malbon, Elizabeth Struthers. "Jonah, Jesus, Gentiles, and the Sea: Markan Narrative Intersections." Pages 251–295 in Geert Van Oyen, ed., *Reading the Gospel of Mark in the Twenty-First Century*. Bibliotheca Ephemeridum Theologicarum Lovaniensium. Leuven: Peters, 2019.

Marshall, I. Howard. *Acts: An Introduction and Commentary*. Tyndale New Testament Commentary. Downers Grove, IL: IVP Academic, 2008.

Martin, Troy W. "Paul and Circumcision." Pages 113–142 in J. Paul Sampley, ed., *Paul in the Greco-Roman World: A Handbook*. Volume One. Revised Edition. New York: T&T Clark, 2016.

McGowan, Andrew. "Animal Acts: Diet and Law in the Acts of the Apostles." Pages 105–120 in Saul M. Olyan, Jordan D. Rosenblum, eds., *Animals and the Law in Antiquity*. Brown Judaic Studies 368. Providence, RI: Brown University, 2021.

Meek, James. *The Gentile Mission in Old Testament Citations in Acts: Text, Hermeneutic, and Purpose*. Library of New Testament Studies 385. Edinburgh: T&T Clark, 2008.

Michael, Matthew. "Yahweh, the Animal Tamer: Jungles, Wild Animals and Yahweh's Sovereignty in the Apocalyptic Space of Daniel 7:1–28." *Scriptura* 119.1 (2020): 1–16.

Milgrom, Jacob. "Of Hems and Tassels: Rank, Authority and Holiness Were Expressed in Antiquity by Fringes on Garments." *Biblical Archaeology Review* 9.3 (1983): 61–65.

Milgrom, Jacob. *Leviticus 1–16*. Anchor Yale Bible Commentary. New Haven, CT: Yale University Press, 1998.

Miller, Chris A. "Did Peter's Vision in Acts 10 Pertain to Men or the Menu?" *Bibliotheca Sacra* 159.635 (2002): 302–317.

Miller, John B. F. *Convinced that God Had Called Us: Dreams, Visions, and the Perception of God's Will in Luke-Acts*. Biblical Interpretation Series 85. Leiden: Brill, 2007.

Miller, Patricia Cox. *In the Eye of the Animal: Zoological Imagination in Ancient Christianity*. Philadelphia: University of Pennsylvania Press, 2018.

Mueller, Eike Arend. Cleansing the Common: A Narrative-Intertextual Study of Mark 7:1–23. PhD diss., Andrews University, 2015.

Moxon, John R. L. *Peter's Halakhic Nightmare: The "Animal" Vision of Acts 10:9 – 16 in Jewish and Graeco-Roman Perspective*. Wissenschaftliche Untersuchungen zum Neuen Testament 432 (Tübingen: Mohr Siebeck, 2017.

Nanos, Mark. "Paul's Reversal of Jews Calling Gentiles 'Dogs' (Philippians 3:2): 1600 Years of an Ideological Tale Wagging an Exegetical Dog?" *Biblical Interpretation* 17 (2009): 448–482.

Nielsen, D.C. Franciso J. Calderon. "Fallow Effects on Soil." Pages 287–301 in Jerry L. Hatfield, Thomas J. Sauer, eds. *Soil Management: Building a Stable Base for Agriculture*. Madison, WI: American Society of Agronomy, 2011.

Nock, A.D. *Early Gentile Christianity and Its Hellenistic Background*. New York: Harper and Row, 1964.

O'Brien, Peter T. *The Epistle to the Philippians*. New International Greek Testament Commentary. Grand Rapids, MI: Eerdmans, 1991.

O'Connor, M. John-Patrick. *The Moral Life According to Mark*. Library of New Testament Studies 667. New York: T&T Clark, 2022.

Oliver, Isaac W. *Luke's Jewish Eschatology: The National Restoration of Israel in Luke-Acts*. Oxford: Oxford University Press, 2021.

Oliver, Isaac W. "Simon Peter Meets Simon the Tanner: The Ritual Insignificance of Tanning in Ancient Judaism." *NTS* 59.1 (2012): 50–60.

Olson, Daniel C. *A New Reading of the Animal Apocalypse of 1 Enoch: 'All Nations Shall be Blessed.'* Studia in Veteris Testamenti Pseudepigrapha 24. Leiden: Brill, 2013.

Oswalt, J. N. "Theology of the Pentateuch." Pages 845–859 in T. Desmond Alexander, David W. Baker, eds., *Dictionary of the Old Testament: Pentateuch.* Downers Grove, IL: IVP Academic, 2003.

Pao, David. *Acts and the Isaianic New Exodus.* Eugene, OR: Wipf & Stock, 2016.

Park, Sejin. *Pentecost and Sinai: The Festival of Weeks as a Celebration of the Sinai Event.* Library of Hebrew Bible and Old Testament Studies 342. Edinburgh: T&T Clark, 2008.

Parsons, Mikeal C. "Nothing Defiled AND Unclean: The Conjunction's Function in Acts 10:14." *Perspectives in Religious Studies* 27.3 (2000): 263–274.

Pervo, Richard I. *Acts: A Commentary.* Hermeneia. Augsburg: Fortress Press, 2008.

Peterson, David G. *The Acts of the Apostles.* Pillar New Testament Commentary. Grand Rapids, MI: Eerdmans, 2009.

Procházková, Ivana. *The Torah/Law is a Journey: Using Cognitive and Culturally Oriented Linguistics to Interpret and Translate Metaphors in the Hebrew Bible.* Prague: Karolinum Press, 2022.

Price, Max D. *Evolution of a Taboo: Pigs and People in the Ancient Near East.* Oxford: Oxford University Press, 2021.

Regev, Eyal. "Jewish Legal Practice and Piety in the Acts of the Apostles: Apologetics or Identity Marker?" Pages 126–143 in Alberdina Houtman, Tamar Kadari, Marcel Poorthuis, Vered Tohar, eds., *Religious Stories in Transformation: Conflict, Revision, and Reception*. Jewish and Christian Perspectives 31. Leiden: Brill, 2016.

Sasson, Jack M. "Circumcision in the Ancient Near East." *Journal of Biblical Literature* 85.4 (1966): 473–476.

Schreiner Thomas R. *The King in His Beauty: A Biblical Theology of the Old and New Testaments*. Grand Rapids, MI: Baker Academic, 2013.

Schwartz, Seth. *Imperialism and Jewish Society: 200 B.C.E to 640 C.E.* Princeton, NJ: Princeton University Press, 2001.

Scott, David R. "The Book of Jonah: Foreshadowings of Jesus as the Christ." *BYU Studies Quarterly* 53.3 (2014): 161–180.

Scott, James M. *Exile: A Conversation with N. T. Wright*. Downers Grove, IL: IVP Academic, 2017.

Seow, Choon-Leong. *Ecclesiastes: A New Translation with Introduction and Commentary*. Anchor Yale Bible Commentary. New Haven: Yale University Press, 1997.

Shnabel, Eckhard J. *Acts*. Zondervan Exegetical Commentary of the New Testament 5. Grand Rapids, MI: Zondervan Academic, 2012.

Solberg, R. L. *Torahism: Are Christians Required to Keep the Law of Moses?* Revised Edition. Franklin, TN: Williamson College Press, 2019.

Solberg, R. L. *What God Has Made Clean: Why Christians Are Not Required to Keep Kosher*. Nashville, TN: Boyle & Co. Publishing, 2023.

Staples, Jason A. "'Rise, Kill, and Eat': Animals as Nations in Early Jewish Visionary Literature and Acts 10." *Journal for the Study of the New Testament* 42.1 (2019): 3–17.

Stendahl, Krister. "The Apostle Paul and the Introspective Conscience of the West." *Harvard Theological Review* 56.3 (1963): 199–215.

Stol, Marten. *Women in the Ancient Near East*. Boston: Berlin: De Gruyter, 2016.

Stiles, Steven James. J*esus' Fulfillment of the Torah and Prophets: Inherited Strategies and Torah Interpretation in Matthew's Gospel*. Wissenschaftliche Untersuchungen zum Neuen Testament 594. Tübingen: Mohr Siebeck, 2023.

Stuart, Douglas. *Hosea–Jonah*. World Bible Commentary 31. Grand Rapids, MI: Zondervan Academic, 1987.

Svartvik, Jesper. *Mark and Mission: Mk 7:1–23 in its Narrative and Historical Contexts*. Coniectanea Biblical New Testament Series 32. Stockholm: Almqvist & Wiksell, 2000.

Thiessen, Matthew. *Contesting Conversion: Genealogy, Circumcision, and Identity in Ancient Judaism and Christianity*. Oxford: Oxford University Press, 2011.

Thiessen, Matthew. "Gentiles as Impure Animals in the Writings of Early Christ Followers." Pages 19–32 in Michal Bar-Asher Siegal, Wolfgang Grünstäudl, Matthew Thiessen, eds., *Perceiving the Other in Ancient Judaism and Early Christianity*. Wissenschaftliche Untersuchungen zum Neuen Testament 394. Tübingen: Mohr Siebeck, 2017.

Thiessen, Matthew. *Jesus and the Forces of Death: The Gospels' Portrayal of Ritual Impurity within First-Century Judaism*. Grand Rapids, MI: Baker Academic, 2020.

Thiessen, Matthew. *A Jewish Paul: The Messiah's Herald to the Gentiles*. Grand Rapids, MI: Baker Academic, 2023.

Tucker Jr., Dennis. *Jonah: A Handbook on the Hebrew Text*. Baylor Handbook on the Hebrew Text. Waco, TX: Baylor University Press, 2018.

Turner, Max. *Power From on High: The Spirit in Israel's Restoration and Witness in Luke-Acts*. Eugene, OR: Wipf & Stock, 2015.

van Bekkum, Koert, Jaap Dekker, Henk van de Kamp, Eric Peels, eds., *Playing with Leviathan: Interpretation and Reception of Monsters from the Biblical World*. Themes in Biblical Narrative 21. Leiden: Brill, 2017.

van Maaren, John R. "Does Mark's Jesus Abrogate the Torah? Jesus' Purity Logion and Its Illustration in Mark 7:15–23." *Journal for the Jesus Movement in its Jewish Setting* 4 (2017): 21–41.

van Maaren, John R. The Gospel of Mark within Judaism: Reading the Second Gospel in its Ethnic Landscape. PhD diss., McMaster University, 2019.

Wahlen, Clinton. "Peter's Vision and Conflicting Definitions of Purity." *New Testament Studies* 51.4 (2005): 505–518.

Wall, Robert W. "Peter, 'Son' of Jonah: The Conversion of Cornelius in the Context of Canon." *Journal for the Study of the New Testament* 29.9 (1987): 79–90.

Way, Kenneth C. *Donkeys in the Biblical World: Ceremony and Symbol*. History, Archaeology, and Culture of the Levant 2. Winona Lake, IN: Eisenbrauns, 2011.

Wenham, Gordon J. *Numbers: An Introduction and Commentary*. Tyndale Commentary on the Old Testament. Downers Grove, IL: InterVarsity Press, 2008.

Wilber, David. *Remember the Sabbath: What the New Testament Says About Sabbath Observance for Christians*. Clover, SC: Pronomian Publishing, 2022.

Wilber, David. *How Jesus Fulfilled the Law: A Pronomian Pocket Guide to Matthew 5:17–20*. Pronomian Pocket Guide Series. Clover, SC: Pronomian Publishing, 2024.

Williams, Logan. "The Stomach Purifies All Foods: Jesus' Anatomical Argument in Mark 7.18 – 19." *New Testament Studies* 70 (2024): 371–391.

Wilderberger, Hans. *Isaiah 28–39: A Continental Commentary.* Translated by Thomas H. Trapp. Minneapolis: Fortress Press, 2002.

Witherington III, Ben. *The Acts of the Apostles: A Socio-Rhetorical Commentary.* Grand Rapids, MI: Eerdmans, 1997.

Woods, David B. "Interpreting Peter's Vision in Acts 10:9–16." *Conceptus* 13.3 (2012): 171–214.

Yong, Amos. *Mission After Pentecost: The Witness of the Spirit from Genesis to Revelation.* Grand Rapids, MI: Baker Academic, 2019.

Young, David M., Michael Strickland. *The Rhetoric of Jesus in the Gospel of Mark.* Minneapolis: Fortress Press, 2017.

www.ingramcontent.com/pod-product-compliance
Lightning Source LLC
Chambersburg PA
CBHW060323050426
42449CB00011B/2627